ELVIS

Other titles in the Weidenfeld & Nicolson *Lives* series include:

ELVIS
BOBBIE ANN MASON

Weidenfeld & Nicolson
LONDON

First published in Great Britain in 2003 by
Weidenfeld & Nicolson

First published in USA in 2003 by Viking/Penguin

© 2003 Bobbie Ann Mason

A CIP catalogue record for this book is
available from the British Library

ISBN 0 297 82979 3

Typeset by Selwood Systems, Midsomer Norton

Printed by Butler & Tanner Ltd, Frome and London

Weidenfeld & Nicolson

The Orion Publishing Group Ltd
Orion House
5 Upper Saint Martin's Lane
London
WC2H 9EA

To Roger

CONTENTS

INTRODUCTION

ON 16 AUGUST, 1977, when I learned that the King – Elvis Presley – was dead, I was vacationing in Nova Scotia. In the lounge at the inn where I was staying, the news came on TV. Stunned, I could only mumble some clichés. The bartender recalled the death of the actor Audie Murphy, a war hero of his generation. I felt far from home. Although I hadn't thought much about Elvis lately, I now sensed there was a great hole in the American cultural landscape. Elvis had always been there, hovering in the national psyche, his life punctuating our times – his appearances on *The Ed Sullivan Show*, his first movie, the death of his mother, the Army, his marriage, the 1968 'Comeback Special'. It seemed inconceivable that Elvis – just forty-two years old – was gone.

For me, Elvis is personal – as a Southerner and something of a neighbour. I heard Elvis from the very beginning on the Memphis radio stations. Many parents found Elvis's music dangerously evocative, his movements lewd and suggestive – but when my family saw Elvis on *The Ed Sullivan Show*, singing 'Ready Teddy', my father cried, 'Boy, he's good!' We had been listening to rhythm-and-blues late at night on the radio for years, and we immediately recognized what Elvis was about. We had heard Arthur 'Big Boy' Crudup and Little Junior Parker and Big Bill Broonzy and Wynonie Harris and Elmore James. In the daytime we listened to big bands, pop hits, country, the opera, everything we could find on the dial. On Sundays we sang in church along with the congregation, and we heard plenty of gospel music – especially the Blackwood Brothers, who influenced Elvis so much. Elvis listened to the same regional stew, seasoned by the far-ranging reach of the radio, so when he emerged with his own startling, idiosyncratic singing style, we recognized its sources.

Elvis was great, so familiar – and he was ours! I don't remember the controversy he stirred up because everything he did seemed so natural and real, and he was one of us, a country person who spoke our language. It was hard to grasp how revolutionary his music was to the rest of the world. And it was years before we could realize what a true revolution in American culture Elvis had ignited.

But now the King was dead. Two writer friends of mine dropped everything when they heard the news and rushed to Graceland, Elvis's Memphis home, to grieve with the multitudes of fans. One of the writers snitched a rose from a floral wreath and still has it displayed under glass on her wall. The other helped himself to the newspaper that had arrived at Graceland the day after Elvis died – the paper Elvis would have read if he had lived. Elvis, who was taken seriously in a wide variety of circles, inspired such a need for connection. He mattered deeply to many different kinds of people. After his death, the world absorbed the story – the utter loneliness of his life, his grasping for ways to ease his pain and sorrow. It was a sad – in some ways a sordid – story, hard to take. Then the grief gave way to a nervous national joke throughout the eighties. Elvis had been part of American life, and now it seemed people didn't quite know what to do about him. Elvis was ridiculed, reduced to a caricature in a sequined jumpsuit. In 1992, the post office held a contest to vote on the new Elvis stamp; we could choose between the young, pretty Elvis and the older, bejewelled Elvis. Of course we chose the pretty one.

Some people refused to accept the news of his death. Sightings were reported. He became a barometer of the culture, a sort of hillbilly voodoo doll. As in life, Elvis was both revered and reviled. In 1980, a scurrilous biography portrayed him as a redneck with savage appetites and perverted mentality, and of no musical significance to American culture. This character assassination undoubtedly helped promote the national joke. Many may have found it preferable to reduce Elvis to a symbol, because Elvis made them uncomfortable. For some, he represented the dark forces, a crude creature from the lower classes; for others, he represented innocence, and the destruction of innocence is an unbearable sight. Perhaps joking about him – transmogrifying him into a fat, drug-crazed hillbilly with gargantuan appetites – both alleviated the guilt and conveniently removed him as a subject for serious examination. But the nineties produced a steady stream of reconsiderations of Elvis. Peter Guralnick's thorough two-volume biography helped to rescue Elvis's reputation and restore an understanding of his music. Guralnick sympathetically portrayed a life that he called an American tragedy.

A few months after Elvis died, I visited the small two-room house in Tupelo, Mississippi, where he was born. It was now a museum, outfitted as it might have been when the Presleys lived there. It was furnished with flea-market antiques – Jesus figurines and heart-shaped pincushions, a washtub, a washboard, a pie safe, a kerosene lamp, and dishes that had come free in detergent boxes during the Depression. But what mesmerized me was the glitter poster – glitter spilled on felt paper, forming the shape of Jesus, with a Bible verse. I hadn't seen one of those since childhood. I remembered them from church. The poster evoked a powerful memory – this fake relic, this reminder of the innocent, religious rock-and-roll artist who became a superstar like the world had never seen before. In the glitter you could imagine the foreshadowing of the sequined jumpsuit. The glitter poster, once ubiquitous in the South, was a little bit of fancy in a drab world. And it embodied immense hope.

MARVEL

ELVIS PRESLEY SEEMED to have sprung on the world without a history. His emergence in the mid-fifties was so sudden, his music so fresh, his personality so evocative that he could not be labelled. People went crazy. There has never been a mania quite like it. Teenagers went wild with excitement; their parents went wild with anxiety over Elvis's overt sexuality. Girls ripped his car apart; they stripped his clothes off; they were ready to rock and roll. Elvis's celebrity was an amazing American phenomenon, and the entire nation was gripped by it. Popular TV variety-show host Ed Sullivan at first found Elvis so shocking he declared he 'wouldn't touch him with a ten-foot pole'. Outside the South, the public found him frighteningly uncouth – a redneck from a backward, bigoted region. His music clearly had an affinity with rhythm-and-blues, from black culture. People heard raw jungle rhythms in his music – voodoo doings.

On the other hand, Elvis swept up marginal groups of people with a promise of freedom, release, redemption; he embodied a yin and yang of yearnings; he took people close to the edge and brought them back again; with his stupendous singing talent, he blended all the strains of popular American music into one rebellious voice; like Walt Whitman, he was large – he contained multitudes; he created a style of being that was so distinctive it could be made into an icon; he violated taboos against personal expression and physicality; he opened the airwaves to risk and trembling. Rock-and-roll had been brewing for years, but its defining moment was Elvis.

Even though he was controversial, his popularity was huge from the beginning, and over the years he became entrenched in American culture. He had eighteen number-one hits in a row; his album of million-selling gold records itself sold a million records; fifty-four million people watched his first appearance on *The Ed Sullivan Show*, an 82.6 per cent share of the nation's viewing audience. In 1956, the year he became known nationally, he became a millionaire, with ten songs on *Billboard*'s Top 100, more than any other artist in the past. His ascendance from regional star to national star to Hollywood all occurred in an eyeblink. He was a boy wonder, both endearing and threatening, with a talent that defied category. Elvis set in motion a style of music that would dominate the world for the rest of the century. It was the beginning of youth culture – kids got their own record players and radios. It was the breakdown of sexual inhibition, and the end of racial segregation.

Elvis's success – and the rock-and-roll revolution – punctured the balloon of 1950s serenity and conformity. America was sunk in its Eisenhower torpor. With its worry about the Soviets and H-bombs, the nation at large seemed desperate for sweet contentment. But race issues were on the boil. The Supreme Court had ruled against segregation in *Brown v. Board of Education* only a few weeks before Elvis made his first record in 1954. The time was right for a magical figure to burst forth like a natural symbol of integration. Black musicians praised Elvis for helping their own music to reach a commercial audience. Little Richard, the inimitable purveyor of 'Tutti Frutti', said, 'I thank God for Elvis Presley. I thank the Lord for sending Elvis to open the door so I could walk down the road, you understand?'

Later, Black Panther leader Eldridge Cleaver, in *Soul on Ice*, credited Elvis with sparking the social revolution of the sixties. Presley 'dared to do in the light of day what America had long been doing in the sneak thief anonymity of night – consorted on a human level with the blacks'.

Popular music began to challenge conventional tastes, and music with a beat – such as Jerry Lee Lewis's 'Whole Lotta Shakin' Goin' On' and Buddy Holly's 'That'll Be the Day' – began to dominate the charts. Because of his suggestive movements onstage, Elvis was called 'Elvis the Pelvis', a name that embarrassed him. He was excoriated for lewdness and lasciviousness. One headline called him the 'self-winding singer'. His hip-swiveling was denounced far and wide, but he professed innocence. He didn't mean anything dirty by it, he said. It was just natural to him to let loose and express what he felt. With his coy lip curl and his playful habit of interrupting his songs to mug or joke, he reminded us not to take him too seriously. Elvis always had a sense of humour about his persona, acknowledging the absurdity of his fame.

Still, the weight of it affected his performance: his behaviour was self-conscious, self-deprecating. Every person who achieves any degree of fame experiences some disorientation, but for Elvis it was unique. In the history of the world, few individuals have had such great success and fame so suddenly, with such far-reaching consequence and with so little preparation for dealing with it. This is a startling thought. How did he bear the burden?

In wondering whether anyone else has ever experienced this sort of sudden global recognition, I can think only of the astronauts walking on the moon. Over two billion people saw the first moon landing. Nearly as many – one and a half billion – saw Elvis in the first satellite-beamed TV show, *Aloha from Hawaii*, in 1973.

Elvis's fame *happened* to him – not entirely unbidden, but in proportions he had not imagined or sought. He was a dreamer, aspiring to stardom. He wanted to be big. He had seen all the movies, heard the songs, knew where the rewards came from – Hollywood and New York, not Memphis or Tupelo. But his desires outweighed his confidence. And his fame socked him in the face. It was as though Elvis himself had made one giant leap and then the whole earth jumped on him for stepping so fancy – jiggling and hunching and gyrating his leg like a brace drill.

The test of the popular hero in our age is his struggle against fame. The personal story of Elvis is his private tussle with his public image as the King of Rock-and-Roll. His tragedy arises from the earnestness of his endeavour to be the superhero he believed he was supposed to be.

TUPELO

THE PRESLEYS WERE country people from East Tupelo, Mississippi, across the railroad tracks from Tupelo. Their neighbourhood was just a few small streets and dirt roads. They spent their lives making do and scraping by – and trying to have some fun. I think of Elvis's parents, Vernon and Gladys, as a pair of cutups – teasing, playing cards, drinking beer, dancing. They were fond of music and loved singing at church. When they eloped, Vernon had to borrow three dollars for the marriage licence, and he was under-age – only seventeen. Gladys was twenty-one. For the record, they both readjusted their ages.

Gladys was gorgeous and slim and crazy about dancing. According to Elaine Dundy's biography, *Elvis and Gladys*, her buck dancing was renowned among her neighbours. In buck dancing, the individual dancer – with eyes closed – somehow relaxes the body until the hips seem to jump out of their sockets so that they swivel and rotate with astonishing looseness. It is as though a subterranean energy has invaded the dancer's body. With her luxuriant dark hair (from her Cherokee ancestor, Morning Dove White) and her languorous manner, she was sexy – perhaps something like Eula Varner in William Faulkner's *The Hamlet*. When she was a teenager, Gladys, like Eula, had spells of lethargy and languidness, her smouldering sexuality throbbing in the Mississippi heat.

When they saw Elvis's gyrations on television in 1956, the neighbours and kinfolks who remembered the way Gladys danced said, 'Elvis got it honest.'

Vernon was a dreamy-eyed, good-looking blond youth – so poor that, as the phrase goes, he didn't have a pot to piss in. He had a reputation for being shiftless, but the Great Depression was on, and Vernon took what work he could get. Gladys, who came from a large family, with a tenant-farmer father and a tubercular mother, had been working hard all her life, farming and sewing. In the late thirties and early forties, she did piecework at a garment factory. Even though she earned only two dollars for a twelve-hour day, going to work at the factory in Tupelo gave her independence, social life, and adventure.

The marriage, in 1933, was impulsive. Vernon was no doubt irresistible, but he had little to offer Gladys. He was too young to have proved himself, and times could not have been harder. Moreover, he was at the bottom of the social scale, and although he had learned carpentry, he could expect few opportunities other than manual labour. In that world, people like Vernon could work hard at whatever came along and still never get anywhere.

When Elvis was born, in 1935, Vernon was driving a milk-delivery route. He owned next to nothing. He worked for others – hoeing corn and peas, sharecropping. His people were farmers, but not landowners. In the rural South, a man owning his own farm was middle-class, even though he might have no cash or luxuries and his survival depended on weather and crop yields and the health of his herds; but survival for people like the Presleys was far more tenuous. They lived in a small, impoverished world where kinfolks were both a burden and a blessing. From time to time after her marriage, Gladys had to depend on the kindness of neighbours and the obligations of kinfolks to help her; and she sometimes had to depend on the government for commodity supplements – a great source of shame.

Elvis was born in a new shotgun-style house Vernon and his brother, Vester, had built with borrowed money on land he didn't own. A shotgun house, of African origin, is a simple, logical design, built on the breezeway principle for cooling the two small rooms. (You could shoot through the front door and straight out the back.) Gladys had been raised in a shack, but although Elvis's birthplace is often called a shotgun shack, it was actually a well-built, lovingly tended home. Gladys, a neat, clean housekeeper, was thrilled to have a place of her own – with such amenities as a wood stove and an outhouse.

On 8 January, 1935, at 4 a.m., Jesse Garon was stillborn, and Elvis Aaron followed at 4:35. As the surviving twin, Elvis was adored and protected, but the stillborn twin remained alive in the Presleys' imaginations. Gladys believed that Elvis carried the strength of both babies. For Elvis, though, as he grew up, it was as if half of him were missing. He felt guilt, wondering even if he might have somehow smothered his twin in the womb, and later on wondering if Jesse had also possessed a talent like his. The loss of the baby – and the inability to have others – made Gladys hold Elvis close to her, indulging him and no doubt causing people to say he was 'spoilt rotten'. Elvis clung to his mother. When she picked cotton, she hauled him along on the foot of her cotton sack. Aware of his parents' hardship, he early developed a reciprocal protectiveness toward them, with the ambition to lead them out of poverty. He was only a small child when he promised his mother a Cadillac one day.

Elvis was born into the mindset of poverty: the deference towards authority and the insolent snarl underlying it, the feeling of inferiority, the insecurity about where the next meal was coming from. Tupelo was a town run by a few old families. In the thirties and forties, the only industries were a dairy (later the home of Borden's Elsie the Cow) and a fertilizer plant. The subtle gradations of status in a small town like Tupelo – with its fine houses downtown and its fringe of outcasts – were as particular as the social nuances in a Jane Austen novel. Elvis always felt out of place when he left the bosom of his family and their social level. When he transferred from his small school in East Tupelo to the larger school in Tupelo, the kids made fun of him and treated him like a country bumpkin, because of the overalls he wore. His family was humble, suspicious, and clannish, their sense of inferiority papered over with pride. The effort to preserve dignity, the struggle against being defined as 'white trash', was a fierce, ongoing drama. Gladys made sure Elvis was always polite. He learned to lower his head with respect when he faced his elders or anyone in authority and to address them as 'sir' or 'ma'am'. She taught him subservience. Like Uncle Tom behaviour for blacks, it was a survival strategy.

Elvis's sense of shame was magnified when his father brought disgrace on the family. He was sent to the state penitentiary, Parchman Prison Farm, along with Gladys's brother, Travis Smith, for altering a cheque. Before the Depression, only blacks received harsh sentences for minor infractions in Mississippi, but this changed, as hunger drove more and more whites to crime. Vernon sold a hog for four dollars, and he and Travis tried to change the cheque into either fourteen or forty dollars. The details are lost now. But Vernon and Travis were caught and made an example of. Vernon was sentenced to three years. At Parchman Farm, a plantation notorious for its exploitation of convict labour, the prisoners were in segregated camps, where they lived on what they could grow. Wearing their striped 'run-arounds', the prisoners ran to the fields at gunpoint and worked from dawn to dusk in the relentless sun almost without let-up. The feared punishment was the lash – a wide strap called 'Black Annie', which was used more often on whites, who tended to be more rebellious than the blacks. Travis's son Billy suspects that Vernon was lashed by Black Annie, noting that Vernon didn't like to go without his shirt in the years after Parchman.

While Vernon was in prison, Gladys and Elvis lived with some cousins in a tiny house in a poor section of Tupelo near the train tracks, where the sounds of the trains were frighteningly close. Gladys was determined to keep the family together. On weekends, she and Elvis travelled on the bus five hours each way to visit Vernon. The pen – a frightful hellhole in most respects – allowed conjugal visiting on Sundays, and Elvis was left to play with other children while his parents disappeared into the 'Red House'. Elvis was three.

The neighbours got up a petition, and Vernon was released from Parchman for good behaviour after eight months. At home, all three Presleys, probably haunted by the Parchman experience, began to suffer from nightmares and sleep-walking. Elvis was a sleepwalker for years, and he continued to have nightmares of abandonment all his life.

Poverty and shame created desire – for attention, for love, and literally for food. Elvis loved hamburgers. When he was a child, he would walk three miles to get a cheap burger at Dudie's Diner. A burger bought at a hamburger joint – the bun soaked with grease, the thin dill coins and an onion slice, all flattened together by the fry cook's spatula and then packaged in a thin waxed paper – was heavenly. You un-wrapped it and wolfed it steaming hot – the tart pickle and sharp onion and tangy mustard mingling and caressing the palate with contradictory flavours. Add a peach Nehi or a chocolate milkshake, more incongruous sensations, and you had bliss. With a burger, a Coca-Cola was a more typical drink – Co'-Cola, the elixir of the South, that sacred formula with the classic taste. The way it burned the throat sharply when you were really thirsty was the height of pleasure.

Elvis craved these sensations, for the Presleys depended on what they could grow and couldn't afford to buy much meat. Something store-bought always seemed superior to the ordinary, everyday home fare. It was the novelty, the special treat. In the rural South, any food that came from the store seemed a release from hardship – almost like getting something for free, since you didn't have to hoe, reap, butcher, or cook it. It always seemed to taste better. At an all-day-singing-and-dinner-on-the-ground at a Southern church, food was celebrated. Eating everything you possibly could hold and then returning for more was in part a way of not letting food go to waste – an imperative. And it was an illusion of freedom – the plenty laid out before your eyes. 'Your eyes are bigger than your stomach' was a rebuke Elvis probably didn't hear often in those days. He cleaned his plate.

Elvis craved hamburgers. He craved attention. He craved music. He craved dangerous things that Gladys wouldn't allow and the church wouldn't allow. A powerful hunger arose in Elvis – for something outside himself, outside poverty, an experience that would authenticate him, say he was somebody.

Gladys indulged Elvis with love and attention, but she was so afraid he would get hurt that she wouldn't let him take risks. 'Stay in the yard!' she would yell out the door. But whenever the sky grew black and the wind picked up, Gladys would swoop her boy into her arms and rush to the storm shelter carved out of a hill some distance away; no doubt she called on the Lord to spare her child. Her fearfulness rubbed off onto Elvis. But a fear of electrical storms is not unreasonable in the rural South, if the buildings are flimsy and the skies wide open and ominous.

When Elvis was a little more than a year old, one of the worst tornadoes in United States history blasted through the heart of Tupelo. Elvis and his parents were at church when storm warnings came, so they hurried into Uncle Noah Presley's school bus and went to his house. The funnel bypassed the Presley household in East Tupelo, but roofs were ripped off, and the Presleys heard the wind and saw the dreadful sky. People claimed that the funnel was so full of lightning the night turned to day. The earth appeared to be a ball of fire, and people thought it was the end of the world. This tornado sounded like a hundred freight trains. It swept one woman up into the vortex, which she reported was completely silent, and she said she could look down at Milam School burning. A black neighbourhood was flung into a lake and disappeared – houses and people and all. In the thirty-two-second sweep, two hundred and sixteen people were killed, over a thousand were injured, and nine hundred homes were destroyed. Mississippi blues singer John Lee Hooker commemorated the tornado in a song. The sound of the awful wind of the tornado would have been unforgettable, and later in the East Tupelo Assembly of God Church – where the congregation gathered its strength after the devastation – the singing would have been earnest, desperate, and loud. The church would have been overflowing with music.

Southern storms affected Elvis's imagination. In grade school, he told a series of stories he had made up about the Tin Man, tales almost certainly derived from *The Wizard of Oz*. With the constant threat of storms, Elvis surely identified easily with the twisting wind that spiralled Dorothy out of Kansas. The threat of lightning storms may also have been behind Elvis's fascination with the Captain Marvel comics, in which lightning bolts symbolize power.

Elvis had tender ears, being subject to ear infections, and he was sensitive to sounds. Besides the frequent roar and blast of storms, he heard the 'lonesome whistle call' of the train, and everywhere he heard people singing and making music. Elvis was nourished by music. At the Assembly of God, the Holiness church his family attended, the style of gospel music was expressive, fervent, joyful, high-spirited. The preacher played the guitar and moved with the rhythm. When he was two, Elvis launched himself out of his mother's lap and ran down the aisle to join the choir. Later, Elvis heard rhythm-and-blues in Shake Rag, the black section of town in the mudflats between his neighbourhood and town. He heard blues and spirituals on the street, in front of the houses, in the churches, at tent revivals. Elvis was always listening. He had some channel in his head hooked up to the divine gods of music. He drank it in; it flowed in his veins like a drug. His love of music was instinctual. He imbibed and saved inside every sound he heard – hymns at church, the popular gospel quartets. On the radio, Elvis heard all the popular music of the day – the wartime big bands, Bing Crosby's world – and even the Metropolitan Opera. Gladys played Enrico Caruso's 'O sole mio' for him on the wind-up Victrolla. Elvis loved it all.

And of course the Presleys always listened to *The Grand Ole Opry* on Saturday nights. Sometimes they had to hook the radio up to their truck battery in order to get the *Opry* on WSM. Country music – songs of heartache, desperation, and longing – dominated white Southern culture. 'Mean Mama Blues' by Jimmie Rodgers was one of Gladys's favourites, and she loved the Louvin Brothers, singers with a typical country sound, a whining croon.

Sometimes on Saturday afternoons Elvis and his family went to the WELO Jamboree at the courthouse, and many times Elvis went alone, so he could hang around a performer called Mississippi Slim. Elvis adored the country singer and shyly asked him questions. And from time to time, Elvis, just a small boy, got up to sing on the radio. Courthouse jamborees – free-for-all live broadcasts of local performers – were common in the South. The region was teeming with fiddlers and pickers and singers. The blues was filtering in from the Delta, just to the west, in cotton country. From the levee projects and the mines, musicians were vocalizing the sorrow of hard lives. Elvis soaked up all the musical sounds around him: the train whistle, the white country singers, the popular songs on the radio, the jamboree performers at the courthouse, the gospel music at his church, the flux of sounds in Shake Rag, the black gospel at the black churches, the tent revivals. He had probably heard the field hollers and work songs of black farm workers, and possibly he even heard them at Parchman State Penitentiary when he went with his mother to visit Vernon. The field hollers – sung to make unbearable work bearable – were gut-pulling primal screams crafted into beautiful cadences and rhythms.

Music was Elvis's true passion, but he was quiet about it. When he was ten, he sang in the statewide contest at the Mississippi-Alabama Fair and Dairy Show at the fairgrounds in Tupelo. He wore glasses and suspenders and had to stand on a stool to reach the microphone. With no musical accompaniment, he sang 'Ole Shep', the Red Foley tear-jerker about a man forced to shoot his old dog. He came in fifth place.

On Elvis's eleventh birthday, Gladys took him to the Tupelo Hardware Store. He intended to buy a .22 rifle with his birthday money, but she talked him into buying a guitar, which was more expensive. She said she would pay the difference. He cried because he wanted the rifle. As usual, Elvis wanted something dangerous and his mother sent him down a safer path. Uncle Vester, who played in honky-tonks, taught Elvis some chords, and Gladys's brother Johnny Smith taught him some more. Frank Smith, the guitar-playing preacher, also helped him and encouraged him to sing in church. In the seventh grade, Elvis took his guitar to school every day. He announced that he would be on *The Grand Ole Opry* some day, and again, the uptown kids made fun of him – a country kid, singing trashy hillbilly music.

The Presleys could have been Faulkner characters. William Faulkner – born only fifteen miles from Elvis – could not have written any set of lives more complicated and layered with tragedy. It is a mistake to think of Vernon, Gladys, and Elvis as simple country people. Country people are rarely simple. Elvis was an innocent, but his life was filled with pain and complex emotion. Nervous energy ran through him, powered by pain – the pain of feeling an outsider, the pain of loss, the agony of material deprivation. The effort to keep from falling off the bottom social rungs into the despair of abject poverty requires an almost gothic desire – and will. The American dream is more urgent when dreamed from near the bottom. It is Sutpen's dream of justice in Faulkner's *Absalom, Absalom*.

Vernon, always looking for work, taking one odd job after another, was at his wits' end over how to provide for his family. Although being an ex-con was not a stigma in his own family and immediate community, it made it more difficult for him to find suitable employment outside of East Tupelo. In 1948, the year they got a record player, when Elvis was thirteen, Vernon moved the family to Memphis, hoping for better prospects there. It was a courageous step, and a fortunate one for nurturing Elvis's talent. Elvis tuned in immediately to the new influences. Memphis was where all the strains of music from the Delta met, on Beale Street. All the great blues singers were born within a hundred miles of Memphis. The convergence of climate, terrain, the railroad, the cotton fields, the levee (a monumental earth-moving project to hold back the Mississippi floods from the fertile Delta), and a history of slavery produced the flood of sound that reached Beale Street.

Black music was heard infrequently on the radio before 1949, when WDIA, in Memphis, adopted all-black programming, but Elvis had many opportunities to hear various kinds of black music before then. Possibly he heard the inventive sounds of bluesmen like Muddy Waters and other singers who listened as Elvis did – holding on to a thread of song, a melody, a stark note of sadness. Elvis heard the heavy beat of Arthur 'Big Boy' Crudup and Big Bill Broonzy and Sleepy John Estes and other performers whose music reflected an urgency, a complex tension between restraint and release, taboo and desire. Elvis listened to music that expressed his desire, his longing, music that assuaged his sense of worthlessness. Music held out a hope – if for nothing other than for music itself.

In Memphis, Elvis saturated himself with music growing from the black experience. He heard the sounds coming from the black neighbourhood across the street from the housing project where he lived. With his cousin Gene Smith, he went to the AME church and sat in the balcony and listened to gospel and spirituals. They played rhythm-and-blues on the jukebox at Charlie's, and they bought outlandish, flashy clothing from Lansky's, a Beale Street clothier that outfitted rhythm-and-blues performers. Elvis, on one of the bottom rungs of society, felt a closer affinity with black people than he did with most whites of a higher status; he shared many cultural similarities with blacks, such as language and food. His only advantage over them was the colour of his skin, and it gave him the privilege of hope, his burning dream of success.

Elvis was born with a unique talent into circumstances that urged the use of it, and with the raw materials at hand to produce something revolutionary. His love of music transcended boundaries. Yet most white people had not crossed the line that Elvis was about to cross. Elvis was a weird, lonely, hyperactive kid, shy and awkward. He was so afflicted with nervous energy that he twitched, his hands beating out rhythms, his legs moving, his feet tapping to sounds in his head. Music gave shape to these twitchings. His sensitivity to sound and rhythm went back all the way through his life – perhaps even to the womb, to the extra heartbeat he heard as his mother's blood pumped through him. Perhaps that echo was always with him, the sound of his twin's heartbeat and womb thrashings. He began his life with a backbeat.

THE SUN SESSIONS

'EVERY ROCK WRITER returns to "That's All Right", as though to the Rosetta stone,' wrote Dave Marsh. He was referring to the history-changing moment in a recording session at Sun Studio in Memphis, Tennessee, on 5 July, 1954, when the talent of Elvis Presley was discovered and realized during the recording of 'That's All Right (Mama)'. It happened so suddenly, it was as if the nebulous, unformed young kid was a genie let loose from a Coke bottle: there he was! Elvis! Before that instant, he was an unfocused, pimply teenager who acted like the cat had got his tongue.

Sam Phillips, the head of Sun Records, had been searching for a unique sound; he wanted the exciting feeling of black music in a white vocalist. He saw a deep kinship between the races, and he had an idea that if he could open up the world of black music, which he was passionate about, to white listeners, it would help promote racial harmony – and it would be a bold musical adventure. He had sensed something in Elvis that he kept trying to coax out – it was the yearning in his voice, Sam thought, a feeling that seemed to come out of his soul. Sam was recording Elvis with Scotty Moore on guitar and Bill Black on bass. During the session, Elvis kept crooning lovesick pop ballads, in the manner of Dean Martin and Bing Crosby. And then it happened. Elvis, full-blown, blasting out 'That's All Right', 5 July, 1954 – the seminal point in rock-and-roll history. But how could this have occurred?

After graduating from Humes High School in Memphis in 1953, Elvis worked at a machinist shop and then on an assembly line manufacturing rocket shells. Early the next year he got a job driving a truck for the Crown Electric Company, with hopes of training to be an electrician. That would be a large step up from his father's work as a 'common laborer', as Elvis had described him. Elvis had little conception of any alternatives to the path of the working stiff. People in his world didn't go to college. It was nothing Gladys or Vernon would have even considered for their son, given their means. And they undoubtedly would have feared that college would create a gulf between them and their boy; he would learn hifalutin words and then look down on his parents. He would move into a realm they didn't under-stand. They would lose him. Yet Gladys insisted that Elvis finish high school – a significant achievement, something she and Vernon hadn't done. After Elvis became famous, someone asked him if he had thought about using his money to go to college, and Elvis reacted as if he had been asked whether he wanted to go to the moon. 'You can't go beyond your limitations,' he said. 'I stay with my own people.'

But even though Elvis knew where he belonged, he was a

dreamer, and he didn't want to labour as his parents did. He fervently wanted to be a gospel singer. A bigger fantasy beckoned to such a dreamer, an outlet that would let him escape his narrow horizons while remaining true to his social class. He could become a big star. Being a star was something he could understand, because he heard stars singing on the radio, and he had seen them in the movies. Their fortunes had nothing to do with higher learning or being born rich. They got paid extravagantly just for entertaining people.

Elvis was the unlikeliest star. He was self-conscious, awkward, nervous. He mumbled. The girl he planned to marry, Dixie Locke, said he was the most easily embarrassed boy she ever saw. He was secretive, afraid of rejection. People had actually told him he couldn't sing. He failed music in high school, and one teacher said she didn't want his kind of voice in her glee club. He was rejected by a gospel quartet he had his heart set on joining. Such rejections confirmed Elvis's sense of inferiority. Yet he was possessed by an urgent sense of possibility. In his own inchoate, boyish, country way, he was on an existential quest to define himself. He experimented and explored; he embraced shifting influences, internalizing them and in his hunger seeking more. Elvis didn't know the power of what he had. Although he lived and breathed music and had been singing all his life, he had little confidence in his own talent. He sang at every opportunity, but he didn't form a band. In the year after high school, he and a buddy or two got little gigs at sock hops and school assemblies and used-car lots. He hung out at all-night gospel singings. He had sung in church all his life, and he had sung with his parents around the piano – Vernon had a strong, mellow voice much like Elvis's voice. But that intimate family singing was different from seeking a livelihood from music. Vernon tried to discourage him, telling him he had never known anyone who made a living from playing a guitar.

Even though he was shy, Elvis had a burning sense of purpose and a desire for recognition. He deliberately drew attention to himself through his appearance. In high school, he grew his hair long and wore ostentatious outfits from Lansky's when other kids dressed in simple, nondescript duds and wore their hair in crew cuts. Of course, they made fun of him. Today we may not realize how gutsy it would have been to wear a bolero jacket or black pants with chartreuse-trimmed pistol pockets to school in the conformist fifties. Elvis's choice of clothing affirmed his marginal status, and it was also an expression of freedom. The shy kid, who often hid in the back row at school, wanted to draw attention to himself. He was an outsider who stressed his apartness by refusing to conform. But at the same time, he courted admiration.

Also, Elvis wore flashy clothes to compensate for his deep dissatisfaction with his looks. Because of his acne, he was extremely self-conscious. He combed his limp, baby-fine hair constantly. His mother even gave him a Toni home permanent once – wrapping locks of his hair in little curl papers like cigarette papers and rolling them on slim plastic rods. Elvis was trying to look like the actor Tony Curtis; still, it is hard to fathom a boy getting a permanent in the fifties. Elvis even wore eye make-up sometimes. A boy in the fifties going to school with a permanent and eye make-up – it defied logic, it was so original and daring. Yet Elvis wasn't effeminate in his appearance or behaviour. He hankered for girls, strutted around like Brando, played football.

When Elvis – all nerves and pimples – went to the Memphis Recording Service, part of Sun Records, for the first time, he claimed he wanted to record a song for his mother's birthday, even though her birthday was two months earlier. Sam Phillips wasn't there, but his associate, Marion Keisker, asked him, 'Who do you sound like?' Elvis replied, 'I don't sound like nobody.' It has always been assumed that Elvis was expressing a confident awareness of his own uniqueness, but it's possible that he was putting himself down. He aspired to join the ranks of mainstream stars like Bing Crosby, but he didn't have the gall to say he sounded like any of them. The song he chose to record (for a four-dollar fee) was 'My Happiness', a sweet Ink Spots ballad with a maudlin recitation in the middle. His voice was interesting enough for Marion Keisker to keep a copy of the recording. Sam Phillips didn't know exactly what sound he was looking for, but he said he would know it when he heard it. There was little reason to think Elvis could make the sound, that half-imagined amalgam of white and black sensibilities. Even though 'My Happiness' was a song popularized by a black group, the sound was remote from Big Bill Broonzy or Howlin' Wolf. The Ink Spots song was bland, and Elvis's rendition was blander still. And yet, beneath the timidity, Marion Keisker could hear something in his voice that suggested to her that Elvis was precisely the singer Phillips was looking for. But it was months before she could persuade him to schedule a session with Elvis at Sun.

Phillips, immersed in the blues from the Mississippi Delta, had a hit with Jackie Brenston's 'Rocket 88', a tune some call the first rock-and-roll record. (There are plenty of other contenders.) And he recorded the Prisonaires, a quartet of prisoners who came to Sun Studio wearing leg chains. Their 'Walkin' in the Rain' was a regional hit, and quieter than the raw blues Sam had been recording. When he began working with Elvis, Sam may have thought he was wasting his time. Elvis was nervous, and the first session fizzled.

'Elvis Presley was probably, innately, the most introverted person that ever came into that studio,' Sam Phillips said in 1978. 'He tried not to show it, but he felt so *inferior*. He reminded me of a black man in that way. His insecurity was so *markedly* like that of a black person.'

Sam hired Scotty Moore and Bill Black to work with Elvis, but they weren't especially impressed with Elvis's singing when they first got together at Scotty's house – Elvis showing up in a lace shirt and pink pants with a black stripe down the legs. Sam scheduled a second studio session anyway – just an experiment, with no need to call in extra musicians.

When Sam asked what he wanted to sing, Elvis was hesitant. He had not considered singing anything unconventional. After consulting with Scotty and Bill about what they all knew, they finally tried 'Harbour Lights'. 'Harbour Lights'! – a 1950 Bing Crosby pop tune. It was as if Elvis was trying to prevent Sam from suspecting what he could really do.

Elvis was too inhibited to reach into his resources and let the raw notes flow forth the way Sam wanted him to do. But Sam didn't hurry him, or try to plant ideas in Elvis's head.

They tried 'Harbour Lights', and they messed around with some other ballads. It was plodding work, but Sam was patient and encouraging. Elvis grew more relaxed.

Then, during a break, Elvis began fooling around with an old Arthur 'Big Boy' Crudup blues tune. The tape recorder was off.

'That's all right, Mama!' Elvis wailed uproariously in a high-pitched, nervous shout.

In the control room, Sam stopped in his tracks. He poked his head through the door and said, 'What are you doing? Back up and try to find a place to start and do it again.' He turned on the tape machine. In this sound, Sam recognized what he was looking for: the energy, the liveliness, the abandon, the risk. Scotty and Bill quickly picked up on Elvis's lead with a forceful, fast rhythm.

And so they did it again. And again and again, until they had it. Where had this music come from? Where had it been hiding? 'That's All Right' seemed like a pop-up from Elvis's secret stash. Elvis seemed to open up, and a startling new music burst through the dam of his self-consciousness. 'That's All Right' wasn't black, it wasn't rhythm-and-blues, arguably it wasn't the first rock-and-roll record. But it was infectious, alive, irreverent. Besides rhythm-and-blues, Elvis threw in country strains and the rhythms of black gospel and the soul of spiritual music, the high-pitched celebrations in the church hymns. He captured the naughtiness and the sadness and the playfulness of both country and blues – two folk styles now blended forever. It was a driving, bluesy, country, rocking synthesis, a combination of many influences, deeply derivative, and totally original.

Elvis, who assumed he couldn't get ahead unless he followed a conventional path, had needed guidance from Sam Phillips, the authority. Elvis didn't seem to have a concept of the creative leap. And yet he made a giant leap, as if by accident, when he was relaxed and not half trying. Elvis wasn't consciously looking for anything except approval – and with it great fame and fortune – but Sam was looking for originality. His great contribution was to grab it when he heard it.

Beneath Elvis's need for approval, Sam observed, was what he called an 'impudence' in Elvis. He liked this. And he admired Elvis's lack of prejudice, his absorption of influences from all directions without judgement. Sam was surprised that Elvis knew a Crudup number, but he soon discovered that Elvis knew it all. He liked Elvis's rebellious streak, the creative energy bursting through that head-down manner. He recognized Elvis's self-effacement, but he also saw a sassy, complex person underneath.

Sam Phillips lost no time in getting 'That's All Right' played on the radio. He took it to his friend Dewey Phillips (no relation), a white DJ, a jumping-jive, fast-talking hep cat who played what were then called 'race records' on WHBQ's *Red Hot & Blue*. He introduced the song abruptly, following some advertising patter that concluded with something like 'Get yourself a wheelbarr' load of mad dogs, run 'em through the front door, and tell 'em Phillips sent you!' As he played the song, the telephone calls began. Elvis had been too nervous to listen to the radio that night, for fear of ridicule, so he told his parents to listen and went to the movies with his cousin Gene Smith. He was hiding there in the dark when Dewey Phillips called the Presley house, demanding an interview with the singer, pronto. Gladys and Vernon, spurred by a man on the radio – an authority figure – calling Elvis, ran to the theatre, routed Elvis out of his seat, and hustled him off to WHBQ.

Elvis, tongue-tied, was so nervous that Dewey decided to keep the mike open and do the interview while letting Elvis think they were just chatting off-mike. Dewey made a point of asking where Elvis had gone to school – Humes High – so his listeners would know Elvis was white. Elvis said mostly 'Yes, sir' and 'No, sir'. That night, Dewey played the song fourteen times, and the calls kept coming. Some listeners were outraged, most were exultant.

Elvis was an overnight phenomenon in Memphis. The record resisted classification. People didn't know if it was rhythm-and-blues, country, or what. Whatever it was, listeners clamoured for it. Many people said Elvis sounded black, like the sounds of the race records. In an era when daytime radio was dominated by tepid crooning, quirky novelty, and chirpy innocence, here was a record – by a white boy – that had the flavour of juke-joint music. It had the thumping abandon, the driving energy, of the life force itself – a thrusting and writhing and wallowing and celebration.

Elvis had crossed a line. White people didn't usually emulate people they were taught to regard as their inferiors. But Elvis had undeniably learned from black musicians, and even though he drew on a wide variety of influences, his music clearly owed a large debt to rhythm-and-blues. Elvis said, 'I like the lowdown songs of Big Bill Broonzy.' And he said later, 'I always heard music with a beat.' Elvis had kicked up a storm that would eventually swell into a national controversy. He did so innocently, without intention or design. He crossed the boundary purely and simply because he could feel the music. Actually, Elvis was expressing a shared class and regional bond with an audience of poor whites and blacks. Rather than making black music or white music or a white imitation of black music, he was making music that was the voice of the Southern poor – both black and white working-class groups. 'In their indigence and low social standing, poor people in the South, both black and white, shared a common heritage that stamped them as outsiders,' writes the historian Michael Bertrand in *Race, Rock, and Elvis*. Part of that heritage was a love of music that rose keening from the gut.

In the South, the working classes were hearing something familiar, something that spoke for them. They heard Elvis's high-pitched wail, his sexual energy, his affirmation, his rollicking drive, his good humour – all of these positive qualities. He was saying *they* were 'all right, Mama'; he was authenticating their lives.

On that memorable night when 'That's All Right' was first broadcast in Memphis, Sun Records had a huge hit – potentially. But the record was not yet in the stores. In fact, Elvis hadn't even recorded a B side yet. Sam rushed Elvis back into the studio, and they scrambled to come up with another song. The surprise choice was 'Blue Moon of Kentucky', Bill Monroe's bluegrass signature tune. Again, Elvis drew on styles from every direction. He charged it up, and Sam added a slapback technique he had created, a home-made echo effect done with two tape machines. Now they had a real record, and Sam began peddling it to radio stations in the South. Elvis's girlfriend, Dixie, had been on vacation with her family and knew nothing about Elvis's recording sessions. She was stupefied when she heard 'Blue Moon of Kentucky' on the radio as soon as she got back from Florida. She hadn't even realized that Elvis harboured professional ambitions. When she'd left, Elvis had been a truck driver with vague musical dreams. Now, overnight, he was a hot, rising showbiz sensation.

In the next year and a half, Elvis recorded more daring, rousing songs for Sam Phillips. From Sam, Elvis learned the discipline of the artist – the patience to translate his passion into quality work. He recorded 'Mystery Train', 'Good Rockin' Tonight', 'Milk Cow Blues Boogie', 'Baby, Let's Play House', and several others. The pleading falsetto on 'Milk Cow Blues Boogie' seems to come straight from Josh White, a black bluesman who was singing the song the year Elvis was born. With Scotty and Bill, Elvis created the Sun sound. Scotty Moore initially sported a finger-picking style of guitar like that of Chet Atkins, but Sam urged him into a different direction, emphasizing rhythm. Bill Black was not a great bass player, but he could slap it in just the right way. The three musicians, working with Sam, rapidly created several records that are now considered classics, records that have changed the course of American music.

It is widely felt that in the Sun sessions Elvis is most authentic. Later in his life, Elvis himself looked back on these sessions and thought they sounded funny. In 1968, he said the recordings sounded like 'somebody banging on a bucket lid'. By then, he had moved in other musical directions. His sights did not linger on 'Good Rockin' Tonight' and 'Milk Cow Blues Boogie'. But Elvis could never again quite capture the rawness of his first records. The sounds that came hurtling out of Elvis's unfettered soul were so real and refreshing – it was as if some juke joint had opened up and racial harmony were a happy reality.

CREATING ELVIS

WHEN DEWEY PHILLIPS first played 'That's All Right', the flurry of excitement was a response to the sound, not to a visual image. The sound was energizing, familiar and yet not familiar – suggesting a venture into forbidden territory. In the studio, Sam Phillips had no idea how Elvis would present himself on a stage. Elvis had acne and a cowlick, and he tended to stammer. During one of his first public performances of the new record, at Overton Park in Memphis, he was so nervous he shook. To steady himself, he rose up on the balls of his feet, but his legs still vibrated, keeping time with the music. His lips involuntarily twisted into a sneer. He was terrified. When the girls began screaming, he was afraid they were making fun of him. He didn't realize they were excited by the shaking going on inside his pleated pants, which whipped like laundry in a wind. But gradually he figured out what was happening, so he put a little more deliberate force into his movements, and the girls screamed more. Elvis realized he had a model to follow. 'Big Chief' Jim Wetherington, a member of Elvis's favourite gospel group, the lively, upbeat Statesmen, jiggled *his* legs and made women swoon, so now Elvis let loose. In subsequent performances, as Elvis began rotating his left leg, and then playing more and more on the reaction he got, his inhibitions exploded.

During the last half of 1954 and the year of 1955, while touring through the South with Scotty and Bill as the Blue Moon Boys, Elvis tapped his hidden resources and mastered his craft. He was moving freely, exploring, discovering, jolting himself out of his cage. He was brimming with sexual energy, and the stage allowed him to give that energy free, exuberant play. Offstage, he was polite, unassuming, insecure, with a burning need for people to like him – and also a burning lust for the young women who clustered around him. He was a sex pistol. He was not only making original, unforgettable music, he was fashioning himself. The creation of the image of Elvis is one of the more astonishing transformations in musical history.

Elvis turned out to be a great natural showman – spontaneous onstage, with an easy rapport with the audience and a sense of what they wanted and needed. With that assurance, he could move extravagantly, his raunchiness arousing raw reactions. In the early days, he was often crude onstage, telling off-colour jokes and gesturing lewdly. He spat. Oblivious to the rules of professional showmanship, he hammed it up with a teenage rebellious energy and a country innocence, throwing decorum to the wind.

There are hardly any fragments of film portraying the early Elvis. People described him as behaving wildly, agog at the commotion he was creating. He was a sight to see. His hair was unconventionally long, wafted up into a pompadour, and he sported sideburns. He wore a colourful shirt, baggy pants, a narrow belt, a loose jacket, and buckskin shoes. Or he wore pink pants with a black shirt, or perhaps purple pants with a green shirt. By mid-1955 he was playing a D-28 Martin guitar with a tooled-leather cover bearing his name. He banged his guitar so fervently he often broke the strings. He worked so hard that backstage afterwards he would douse his head under a cold faucet and then shake it like a big dog. One imagines the gleeful abandon he felt; it was an awakening to power and opportunity, a burgeoning confidence in his music, and a release of sexual vitality that Elvis lost no time in putting to the test on the road trips. He was like a young stud at a rodeo, Scotty Moore said. After a show Elvis would often stand behind a table at the stage door. 'The girls would swarm, and he'd kiss every one and run his hands all over them, and they'd giggle,' recalled Paul Yandell, a guitarist with the Louvin Brothers, who toured with Elvis. Yandell once saw Elvis go after a pretty girl who was talking in a telephone booth. 'He opened the door and grabbed her by her breast. She slapped him silly!'

Yandell said, 'Elvis would walk onstage and he'd wiggle or move his leg or his hand and they'd squeal. The girls would shout out requests, and he'd say, "I'm gonna do what I want to do first and then I'll do what you want me to do." ' There was a bit of petulance and cockiness in Elvis's voice as he toyed with his audience. He performed with quick gestures. He would bend both knees slightly – but very fast, then stop. Yandell said, 'He'd do something with his finger and they'd scream. It was so funny. He'd be roaring along and he'd suddenly freeze – for fifteen seconds. And they'd scream and scream. And then he'd go back to roaring along. And then he'd freeze again. He'd do it for meanness! But he couldn't help moving the way he did. He had to move with the music.'

And he seemed to be double-jointed, the way he could bend his fingers back all the way to his forearm. His movements had the effect of shock, humour, playfulness, and unmistakable sensuality. Elvis pretended his leg had a mind of its own, and he'd try to make it 'behave'. He kicked one leg out at an odd angle and balanced it on his toe, perpendicular to the floor, then watched it whirl. As he sang, holding his guitar across his hips, he stood with his feet planted far apart, knees bent, as if anchoring himself for a spectacular launch.

This pose has shaped the rock-and-roll musician's persona ever since, but it comes from a much older tradition. In African-American dance, the stance is always wide-legged, an imitation of the position of the labourer. Africans did not use animals or wheels for labour; it was done entirely by the unaided human body. The worker spread his legs, bent his knees, and swayed rhythmically in order to shift and lift a heavy load. Alan Lomax, in his book on Delta blues, *The Land Where the Blues Began*, tells us that this rhythm was called rocking, and that rocking is a root of African-American music and dance. The old spiritual 'Rock, Daniel' was a way of preserving African dance during times of slavery by performing it in church. The labourer's rocking, during performance, is transformed into a sexual dance. By adopting this ritual movement, Elvis was removing himself from poverty through his music, and he was celebrating by moving freely, rhythmically, with joyful, sensual rhythm, breaking loose from the destiny of heavy labour that he was born to. In playing their music, he was identifying with black people, with whose cultural heritage he had so much in common. He was suggesting that the powerful taboos separating them were only illusory.

His mostly white, Southern working-class audience knew it. They identified with Elvis's style of music. It appealed to the young and unformed with its promises of deliverances, its rebel assault on the brutality of labour, its joyous freedom. Elvis was giving free rein to his love of music – rhythm-and-blues, gospel, country, pop. He was throwing everything in, perfecting the arrangements in the studio with hours and days of work, getting it just right, then on the stage bringing every spontaneous notion to bear on the emotion of the songs. Even in his earliest shows (some of which were tape-recorded), he was experimenting, never doing a song by rote, but shifting intonations and dabbling with the shadings of rich sounds.

His music helped open up access to black music, and in turn many blacks felt that Elvis affirmed their lives. In an interview in 1956, Elvis said, 'The colored folks been singing it and playing it just like I'm doin' now, man, for more years than I know. They played it like that in the shanties and in their juke joints, and nobody paid it no mind till I goosed it up. I got it from them. Down in Tupelo, Mississippi, I used to hear old Arthur Crudup bang his box the way I do now and I said if I ever got to the place where I could feel all old Arthur felt, I'd be a music man like nobody ever saw.' Towards the end of his life, when asked by a Swedish journalist if he had achieved his ambitions, Elvis said, 'I just wanted to be as good as Arthur Crudup.'

Elvis understood his debt to African-American music. But despite his love for the music he was performing – and the riotous acclaim it brought him – Elvis may not have been entirely comfortable with it. A basically diffident guy, he must have felt uneasy at the controversy it was provoking. And no white boy in the South could have been entirely happy about being identified with 'black' music. He must have harboured doubts. How far could he go with this hybrid, jumpy music?

Elvis didn't know what the boundaries were. Nobody did. While *Billboard* magazine tried to keep its charts straight – categories of R&B, pop, country – Elvis's records were hopscotching across these charts. At first WELO in Tupelo refused to play its own native son because it was against its policy to play race records.

Sam Phillips wangled a coveted spot for Elvis on *The Grand Ole Opry* at Ryman Auditorium in Nashville, 2 October, 1954. Three months after cutting his first record, Elvis reached the citadel of country music. He was nervous, and Scotty and Bill even more so; there was a feeling of doom, a fear of mockery and failure. They performed 'Blue Moon of Kentucky', worrying about what Bill Monroe would think of their rocking rendition of his bluegrass classic. The audience response was tepid, but Monroe – the King of Bluegrass – professed that he liked their performance. The *Opry* itself was not especially welcoming. Afterwards, the *Opry* manager decided Elvis wasn't right for the *Opry*. According to some reports, he told Elvis he didn't want any more of that 'nigger music' on his programme and advised him to go back to driving a truck. Elvis was so disheartened that he cried, and on the way home he accidentally left his suitcase at a gas station.

Of course, it was an irresistible opportunity to perform on the *Opry*. Elvis could hardly refuse. But did he really want to be locked into the country music genre, when the musical possibilities he had opened up violated and transcended the conventions of country music? Elvis's true allegiance at this point seems elusive. Did he really want to claim a 'hillbilly' heritage? Elvis throughout his life tried to dissociate himself from the pea-patch poverty of his country origins. Although his music is always said to be a mix of country and rhythm-and-blues, as if it were that simple, Elvis doesn't really sound like Hank Williams or the Louvin Brothers. He may have been following in their footsteps, but he was moving beyond the lonesome whine of country music into high-energy, all-hell-is-breaking-loose rock-and-roll. Flopping on the *Opry* was probably a blessing. Elvis was charting his own course, and adapting to the *Opry*'s standards would have ruined him.

While in Nashville, Elvis had a conversation with Ernest Tubb, one of his country heroes, in which he spoke admiringly of Tubb's music and told him his true ambition was to sing country music. Tubb reported it this way to Peter Guralnick: 'He said, "They tell me if I'm going to make any money though, I've got to sing [this other kind of music]. What should I do?" I said, "Elvis, you ever have any money?" He said, "No, sir." I said, "Well, you just go ahead and do what they tell you to do. Make your money. Then you can do what *you* want to do."'

It was a curious conversation. Did Elvis mean what he said? Or was he sucking up to Tubb? Or did Tubb twist the record to elevate his own style of music? We can't know. Yet the reported conversation resonates. Elvis was uncertain about his direction. When his car had first pulled up in front of Ryman Auditorium, he was disappointed to see how decrepit the place looked. Downcast, he turned to the others in the car and said, 'Is *this* what I've been dreaming about all my life?'

He had not consciously set out to be an innovator. Perhaps when he told Marion Keisker at Sun, 'I don't sound like nobody,' he was lamenting how different he was. Again and again, in the months that followed, he spoke of giving the audience what it wanted to hear. He feared he was only a craze. Did he follow Tubb's advice then, performing what the crowds wanted, while biding his time? When he came to Sun Records, Elvis had wanted to sing ballads; he had always sung ballads. Inadvertently setting off a rock-and-roll revolution was nothing he had designed. It just happened. Yet he loved the music and went with the feeling, gladly receiving the mountain of approval.

After the *Opry*, Elvis and the Blue Moon Boys joined the *Louisiana Hayride*, a country-music show that was less rigid than the *Opry*. They appeared on Saturday nights, in Shreveport, and during the week they traipsed throughout the South on random bookings – places like the Big 'D' Jamboree in Dallas, the Hoedown Club in Corpus Christi, a Pontiac showroom, American Legions, a lot of school-houses. They played at feed mills, using the back end of a truck for a stage. Later, Scotty obtained a special handmade amp (the Echosonic) that had a built-in slap-back effect, enabling him to take the unique Sun Studio sound on the road. Elvis and Scotty and Bill worked steadily touring the South, where their five Sun records were selling well. Elvis quickly became the headliner. Other performers didn't want to follow him on a bill because he stole the show. As he became better known, he became even more controversial, and he got in fights with jealous guys whose girlfriends swooned over him.

The touring was exhausting – tiring, high-tension performances strung between long stretches on the road. Elvis bought a pink Cadillac, but when a wheel bearing caught fire, it burned up, just after an appearance in Hope, Arkansas. Later, Vernon, putting his carpentry to use, built a little plywood trailer (like a rolling outhouse, someone said) to haul the band's equipment. He painted it pink. Eventually, when it had a flat tyre, they abandoned it on the roadside.

Meanwhile Dixie Locke, the girl Elvis had planned to marry, gave up on him. He had soared out of her sights, changed from the quiet, church-loving boy she knew. In truth, Elvis had girlfriends scattered all over the South by now. Gladys continued to worry about her son and couldn't rest easy unless he called her every night. They had arguments over her worry about him, but he dutifully called home.

As Elvis's fame grew throughout the South, he caught the attention of Pat Boone, a Columbia University student and ultra-clean-cut fifties teen idol. Boone had a hit record with a cover version of the Charms' 'Two Hearts', on the Dot label, which specialized in white covers of black songs. He had seen Elvis's name on country jukeboxes in Texas, but he was sceptical of the hype about him. 'I wondered how in the world a hillbilly could be the next big thing, especially with a name like Elvis Presley,' he said. When he introduced himself to Elvis at a show, he was struck by Elvis's lack of eye contact. Elvis talked in 'sort of a country twang mumble', Boone observed. 'He was always looking down, you know, like he couldn't look up.' But Elvis's performance knocked the house down, Boone said. 'Then he opened his mouth and said something, and it was so hillbilly that he lost the crowd. … As long as he didn't talk, he was okay.' Pat Boone, it is worth noting, was the son-in-law of country star Red Foley, whose song 'Old Shep' was the first song Elvis ever sang in public, and who popularized the black gospel song 'Peace in the Valley', which Elvis would eventually sing on *The Ed Sullivan Show*. At this point, Elvis looked up (so to speak, with his head lowered in respect) to Pat Boone because Boone was a national star, while Elvis was just a regional upstart.

In this early period, Elvis was experimenting – musically and personally. Onstage he could transcend his origins. He could communicate without that sense of inferiority that weighed his head down. When he performed, he was confident, in charge. He hit the stage like a tornado. After tasting the glory of success – the success he had dreamed of all along – he was willing to try anything.

THE COLONEL

WHILE ELVIS WAS touring through the South in 1954 and 1955, he was stalked by a waddling hulk who insinuated himself into Elvis's business until eventually he became Elvis's manager. 'Owner' might be more accurate. He lurked around Elvis for months before swooping in to possess him. He went after his prize as if Elvis were a winning thorough-bred, and he treated him thereafter as a commodity. Colonel Thomas A. Parker was his name. The title was honorific and virtually meaningless, but Parker used it insistently, to proclaim his importance. He had cast aside his earlier identity as a Dutch exile (Andreas Cornelis van Kuijk) with-out citizenship in any country – facts Elvis never learned. After coming to America in the twenties, Parker spent the Depression in the carnival circuit of the South. From tent shows, he advanced into country-music promotion – handling Eddy Arnold, then Hank Snow. Believing that Elvis would become a superstar, he was determined to take control of 'the boy', as he called him.

Elvis had a manager, Bob Neal, a Memphis disc jockey,

but the Colonel moved in on this tenuous arrangement by offering to facilitate bookings. He asked Elvis and Neal to sign a contract allowing him to promote Elvis and negotiate fees for concerts. Since Elvis was a minor, he had to get his parents' signatures. The contract itself was shockingly manipulative, written to Parker's advantage in every way. It read like indentured servitude. In effect, Parker owned Elvis's talent. Elvis, unassertive when it came to business, gave the Colonel the authority he didn't trust himself to exert. The contract required Elvis to pay the Colonel twenty-five hundred dollars for his services up front and called for one hundred concert appearances, for which Elvis would receive just two hundred dollars each (to be divided with his musicians) – concerts that had not yet been booked. The Colonel demanded expenses for himself and further payment if Elvis accepted shows the Colonel didn't negotiate. And the agreement was open-ended: the Colonel could reconfigure it at any time, which he did later when Elvis turned twenty-one. Then the Colonel became Elvis's exclusive manager, getting 25 per cent plus expenses.

Whatever else may be said about him, Colonel Tom Parker advanced Elvis's meteoric rise onto the national scene. With almost limitless possibilities opening ahead of him, Elvis needed to be steered towards the best – and most lucrative – choices. Parker was shrewd and relentless in his goal. He was a balding, corpulent man who is invariably described as waddling rather than walking. He wore funny hats and sloppy clothes and smoked cigars. He wore undershirts in public. Boisterous and affable, he talked – literally out of the side of his mouth – with what seemed a strange speech impediment. Actually it was the remnant of his Dutch accent, but nobody knew he was Dutch.

It's easy to view the Presleys' business arrangement with the Colonel in the worst light – the Presleys being victimized by a con man. But signing up with the Colonel was actually a fairly sensible thing for them to do in their situation. Their social class demanded subservience to authorities – employers, people in a higher status. In order to get ahead, or to get out, you had to figure some angles. There had to be a hustle, because you knew the game was rigged against you. A person like Elvis, from East Tupelo, knew he couldn't join the country club in Tupelo or go to dinner at the swank Peabody Hotel in Memphis. He couldn't waltz into the watering holes of the upper echelons on his own merits. He didn't belong in their company and never would – and didn't want to. Even if he became a famous singer, he still wouldn't belong.

The Presleys knew they needed a guide, someone of their own kind who could manoeuvere among the bankers, lawyers, company executives – none of whom were to be trusted. The Presleys probably considered themselves lucky to find a con man who could challenge the big dudes, because they knew the big dudes would just stomp on them. That was the way life was.

The South was full of small-time traders. Every farmer had to figure angles in order to trade his crops and livestock. There was a little of the horse trader in most of these men. They prided themselves on not being taken in, and they also liked to put one over on someone else. It was part of the game. In Faulkner's fictional world, Flem Snopes, the ultimate horse trader, doesn't mind a good swindle. In 'Spotted

Horses', the object of the game is not merely to sell some horses of questionable value, but to make the customers into fools. When the horses turn out to be wild, untamed Indian horses, the customers, who have paid good money for them, are left with the almost impossible challenge of catching their snorting, bucking purchases. A swindle isn't complete without a prank. The Colonel shared this outlook. He was a prankster himself, known for his diabolical sense of fun, and in promoting Elvis he used all the tricks he had learned from the carnival. He never wanted to give full value for the money.

Elvis and his father probably recognized the Colonel – the old carny, as he was often called – as a type of horse trader, and they knew he was good at his work because they could see how smooth he was. He knew how to make deals. Elvis and Vernon probably realized that when you hired someone like that, he would bend things around to his own advantage. They knew he would feather his own nest, but they accepted that because the Colonel would keep unimaginable amounts of money flowing their way. If Elvis made a million dollars, and even if the Colonel swiped half, the remainder was still a fabulous fortune for a guy who had been earning thirty-seven dollars a week driving a truck for Crown Electric.

Vernon himself was something of a trader, parsimonious and careful with a dollar, and accustomed to that manner of doing business. The Colonel had little trouble winning him over – he could see the dollar signs in Vernon's eyes. But Gladys – keeper of dignity and soul in the family – didn't trust the Colonel. She called him a 'fast-talking bullshooter'.

He had to woo her. He was very good at the game. In his own circles, he called himself the Snowman, because at snow jobs he was unexcelled. And the Colonel was dangling the promise of so much money in front of their noses there was really no way for the Presleys to refuse.

If some straight-talking Yankee had come at them, offering to manage Elvis for only 10 or 15 per cent, the Presleys might have been so suspicious of his assertive manner and his Northern accent that they would not have dealt with him. But the Colonel was friendly, charming, and full of whoop-de-do ideas (like hiring an elephant to march through town wearing a sandwich board to advertise Elvis). Even though she agreed to sign, Gladys still reserved her judgement. She was afraid of what would happen to Elvis and the family if he hit the bigtime. Gladys was a warm-hearted woman, and she didn't feel any warmth in Colonel Tom Parker.

Parker moved to acquire Elvis's contract at Sun Records. Dismissing Sam Phillips's label as too small-time, Parker made a deal with RCA Records to buy Elvis's contract from Sun for the unheard-of price of thirty-five thousand dollars. Phillips, who detested the Colonel but needed the money, knew he couldn't produce and market Elvis's records properly – or keep up with his growing fame. Phillips later claimed he had no regrets in giving up his discovery.

When Elvis signed with RCA Victor on 21 November, 1955, a celebratory photograph appeared in the press. Gladys is kissing Elvis on the cheek, her pocketbook held loosely at her side. Behind her, the Colonel, grinning, has his hand on her shoulder. Vernon, on the other side of Elvis, stands straight, facing the Colonel.

The next day Elvis sent a telegram to Colonel Parker. He wrote: 'Dear Colonel, Words can never tell you how my folks and I appreciate what you did for me. I've always known and now my folks are assured that you are the best, most wonderful person I could ever hope to work with. Believe me when I say I will stick with you through thick and thin and do everything I can to uphold your faith in me. Again, I say thanks and I love you like a father. Elvis Presley.'

THE BIGTIME

WITH THE RCA Victor contract in hand, the Colonel knew it was time to take Elvis to New York and alert the nation. In 1956, just a year before Sputnik blasted off from the Soviet Union, Elvis Presley blasted into orbit. It was the Year of Elvis. In much of the South, the excitement was proprietary – if he was on national TV, then his glory was reflected on the whole region.

Elvis made nine appearances on network television programmes in the first half of the year. His first RCA record, 'Heartbreak Hotel', was number one by April, and his first album, out in May, was number one for ten weeks. Elvis went to Hollywood for a screen test and signed a movie contract. He continued to tour – more widely and at larger venues. The nation was agape and the Presleys were goggle-eyed. Money poured in. In only one month, April, Elvis earned about seventy-seven thousand dollars, which was maybe worth half a million in today's dollars – even without benefit of today's hyper-inflation in the entertainment industry. With the management fees and commissions and expenses, Elvis took home less than half – and that was before taxes. Still, it was a fortune. He bought his parents a new house for forty thousand dollars cash. He bought a Cadillac Eldorado Biarritz.

'It's all happening so fast,' Elvis told people at a reception for him in New York. 'There's so much happening to me … that some nights I just can't fall asleep. It scares me.'

Very quickly Elvis was swept up in a whirling storm. His records moved beyond the working class of the South, who found him as familiar as a brother, and reached middle-class young people who responded to the beat and the energy. Outside his familiar territory, he was treated as an exotic, and his popularity soared. *Time* and *Newsweek* trumpeted his phenomenal rise. *Life* splashed the headline 'Howling Hillbilly Success'. Elvis was overwhelmed by all the attention – buoyed, crazed, flying high, inwardly insecure. He told the *Memphis Press-Scimitar*, 'Just because I managed to do a little something, I don't want anyone back home to think I got the big head.'

The rocket ride was bumpy. The controversy over Elvis had been steadily growing, but his performance of 'Hound Dog' on Milton Berle's television programme in June set off a national furore. At the end of the song, Elvis's athletic antics slowed down to a striptease bump and grind. Middle-class, middle-aged America was almost unanimously outraged. Volcanic denunciations erupted. Elvis was vulgar, indecent, a threat to America's youth. Elvis, hurt and angered by the attacks, protested that Debra Paget, who was also on *The Milton Berle Show*, wore a 'tight thing with feathers on the behind where they wiggle most. … Man, she bumped and pooshed out all over the place.' You can hear belligerence in his tone as the attacks mounted. Elvis could not take criticism, and he received a huge amount of it in a very short time. He claimed innocence, defending his style as natural. 'When I sing this rock 'n' roll, my eyes won't stay open and my legs won't stand still. I don't care what they say, it ain't nasty.' Elvis was especially hurt that so many denunciations came from preachers, since he considered himself a God-fearing, moral person. The almost unspoken fear underlying the furore was that Elvis's behaviour crossed racial lines. He was described as primitive and disgusting. The Alabama White Citizens Council denounced 'this animalistic nigger bop'.

The cultural elite pronounced him to be without talent – lacking formal training, tradition, or restraint, he could not be comprehended or condoned. Although many adults were horrified by Elvis, most teenagers loved him. Products of the prosperous, post-war 1950s, they were beginning to find something unfulfilling in the Betty Crocker and *Father Knows Best* world. Elvis amplified their first whispers of dissatisfaction with post-war America. Teenagers had celebrated James Dean in *Rebel Without a Cause* as the expression of the rebel hero. Now they picked Elvis as the new embodiment of the nascent youth rebellion. They bought a million copies of 'Hound Dog' in no time flat, but they had no sense of where that music came from. Elvis was as mysterious to them as he was to their parents.

Elvis differed from his new audience. Though super-charged with riotous energy, he was not resisting the same things his new fans were. He rebelled against poverty, not affluence. He wanted acceptance, not alienation. Elvis aspired to be like James Dean, but not as the misunderstood teenager in *Rebel Without a Cause*. Elvis saw James Dean as someone with a romantic sensibility who was also a successful movie star. Elvis wasn't in the beat tradition and he wouldn't be in the next wave, the hippies. He was a representative of the marginalized who fight their way into the harbour, not the disaffected who jump ship.

After Milton Berle, Elvis was scheduled to appear on *The Steve Allen Show*. Moral guardians urged Allen to cancel. Allen didn't go that far (he knew the value of having America's hottest act on his show), but he promised that Elvis 'will not be allowed any of his offensive tactics'. Allen used an offensive tactic of his own to make Elvis safe for America. To counter Elvis as sexual threat, Allen made Elvis the butt of feeble humour. Elvis, wearing a tuxedo, had to sing 'Hound Dog' to a basset hound – an oxymoron, the rustic trying to be suave. The dog, too, was tux-attired. Although Elvis was a good sport and played along, the effect was ludicrous. And in the skit that followed, Elvis was shown trading cornpone jokes with country yokels – Steve Allen, Andy Griffith, and Imogene Coca got up in rube gear. The country bumpkin, the hapless hayseed, was always good for a laugh, and Allen drew on these images for all they were worth. By twisting Elvis's music, burying it beneath silly antics and stereotypes, he attacked not only the music but Elvis himself. Elvis felt like a fool. Steve Allen had even mispronounced his name: the 's' in Presley is a soft 's', not a 'z'. *The Steve Allen Show* was Elvis's first full-scale encounter with the hollow, inauthentic packaging of TV, and Elvis said later that it was the first time he felt he had sold out.

Elvis knew that what was at issue wasn't just his music and his sexual power but his country-bumpkin image. Early in his career he had been promoted as the Hillbilly Cat, a sobriquet he disliked. Steve Allen could defuse the sex bomb by reducing Elvis to a dismissible Li'l Abner caricature. The insult to Elvis and his family, though, was profound. The Presley family had fought hard against being thought of as hillbillies, a derogatory term that suggested ignorant white trash; they had worked to pay their own way, to get ahead, and to be considered decent. They had striven to overcome the stigma of Vernon's time at Parchman Farm (his imprisonment had been kept from the public). So the manipulation of Elvis on the TV programme was humiliating, although it may not have registered immediately because they were so accustomed to being treated as inferiors. Years later, the Colonel claimed that he was behind the basset-hound-in-tails set-up. For the Colonel, who thought in terms of tricks and show animals, it must have seemed like a good publicity stunt.

In a way, Elvis knew what he was in for. All his life he had known that venturing forth from his station was risky and that he would be vulnerable to degradation and shame. Unfortunately, his innocence – not to say uncouthness – sometimes created the very hick image he wanted to refute. Earlier in the year, when he came to New York City to meet people at RCA, his new label, he wore a lavender ribbon shirt and blue alligator loafers. He greeted the publicity director with an electric buzzer hidden in his hand, the kind of joke a ten-year-old would play. 'He was extremely polite, but he was completely lost,' said Freddy Bienstock, the song publisher.

Over and over, New Yorkers noticed how charming and self-effacing and humorous Elvis was. The executives were impressed. He was a keen observer, a 'quick study', they said. He didn't make the same mistake twice – at least not in social etiquette, when it was so important to him to fit in and behave properly. The electric buzzer didn't go off again. But he was out of his element in New York. People had a superior attitude there. Interviewers found it odd that he expressed his musical ambitions in terms of helping his parents.

The day after the Allen debacle, Elvis went to a recording session. Outside the studio, fans held up placards reading, 'We want the real Elvis' and 'We want the gyratin' Elvis'. Inside the studio, for the first time, Elvis took over control of a session, and he was insistent on getting each song exactly right, recording 'Don't Be Cruel' twenty-eight times and 'Hound Dog' thirty-one. He would later get a reputation for being a perfectionist. Elvis understood what he had to do to maintain his own integrity; he was determined to prove himself, to show up his critics. Maybe he remembered what Sam Phillips had told him when he sold his prodigy's contract to RCA. 'Look, you know how to do it now, you go over there and don't let anybody tell you,' Sam had said. 'They believe enough in you that they've laid some cold cash down, so you let them know what you feel and what you want to do.'

The Steve Allen Show intensified Elvis's insecurities, but it may have proved to be a spur for his new determination for artistic control. He knew his music better than the RCA people did. At an earlier RCA recording session, in Nashville, when Elvis recorded 'Heartbreak Hotel', Chet Atkins had been in charge of the session, but he and Elvis never clicked.

Now Elvis was in charge. What he heard in his head was rich and complicated and full of mystery, and he set to work, translating it into powerful, high-spirited songs. With the 'Hound Dog' session, he in effect became the producer of his own recordings, as Sam Phillips had been at Sun. In one day, Elvis recorded 'Hound Dog', 'Don't Be Cruel', and 'Any Way You Want Me', all of which would become enormously popular and would convey Elvis's energetic spirit to the world, making him the most successful artist in RCA history.

All his life there had been authorities telling him what to do. Now he was free to grow as an artist. He engaged Colonel Parker to make all his business decisions, and the Colonel grandly allowed that he wouldn't interfere in Elvis's personal life or with Elvis as an artist. It was an arrangement that Elvis could not have suspected would later catch him in a trap.

The photographer Alfred Wertheimer travelled with Elvis for several days during this stage of his career – the big year of 1956 – taking over three thousand photographs of Elvis becoming a star, including photos of the RCA session in New York. Elvis was twenty-one, naive, perplexed by his fame – wallowing in it, but also standing back from it. Wertheimer selected many poses that minimize Elvis's nervous energy and adolescent behaviour while capturing his innocence and reserve. Elvis looks wide open but thoughtful. It is almost as if Elvis the Innocent is watching himself become Elvis the Star. He is tentative, baby-faced. The photos are sensual – a beautiful young man ripe for the world.

After the recording session, Elvis returned to Memphis on the train, and Wertheimer accompanied him at his own expense, so that he could document the young idol on his triumphant return to his home town. In a concert at Russwood Park on 4 July, the night of his return, Elvis assured the people of Memphis, 'You know those people in New York are not going to change me none. I'm gonna show you what the real Elvis is like tonight.'

AUDUBON DRIVE

WHEN ELVIS'S TRAIN reached Memphis that Fourth of July, 1956, the conductor let him off near a local station, and Elvis walked almost two miles home. It was one of the last times in his life he could walk down a street without gathering a crowd. He was floating. The Steve Allen tribulation was behind him, he had made some knock-dead recordings, and he was returning – proud, strengthened – to his family.

The house he headed for in the fashionable Audubon Park section of town was new. The family had moved into it in March, and they were still giddy with delight over its grandeur. Elvis wanted his mother to have a comfortable house, with new furniture and a nice place in the back for a vegetable garden. Even when he was a child, Elvis was determined to help his parents out of poverty, and now he had bought them a dream house. The pink Cadillac he long ago promised his mother was in the driveway.

He arrived just as the new swimming pool was being filled – with a garden hose from the kitchen. The pool pump wasn't yet working. Elvis jumped into the pool and splashed with his cousins, even though the water was only a couple of feet deep. Actually, Elvis couldn't swim, but the important thing was having a pool. That day, kinfolks and friends crowded around, milling through the house, celebrating Elvis's success. Fans flocked to the house to gawk. They lined up against a picket fence behind the open carport, watching while the family sat on the patio or played in the pool.

That summer, when I was sixteen, my father took our family to the Memphis Zoo. It was our first trip to a zoo, and we had never travelled to a big city before, so we were in a state of amazement. But what I really had my mind on was: where is Audubon Drive? Everybody knew that Elvis had bought his parents a home on Audubon Drive. The fan magazines displayed picture spreads of it, with Elvis lounging in his pink bedroom among his fan letters and teddy bears. Perhaps I could locate the house by looking for a Cadillac in the driveway. I kept my eyes open.

I didn't dare ask my father to go roaming the streets of Memphis, hunting for Audubon Drive, but we did drive through a nice neighbourhood, and I remember wondering if we were anywhere near Elvis's house and entertaining various fantasies of meeting him. The idea of actually going to a star's house and hanging around for a glimpse seemed absurd, though. We might feel awe if our own relatives or neighbours had somehow produced a famous son, and we would be reluctant to approach them. And wouldn't it be just like them to go buy a Cadillac to show off their new riches? I learned much later that if we had found Audubon Drive and joined the cluster of fans who camped there regularly, Gladys might have come out in her housecoat with a plate of cookies and maybe even invited us in. Elvis might have even appeared, behind the wheel of one of his Cadillacs. And they would have been down-to-earth, nice, plain folks. Everyone said so.

The Presleys' new house, their first real home since Vernon built the little house Elvis was born in, was a splendid ranch house – a four-bedroom dream home. Today a ranch house seems ordinary and modest, but at the time it probably seemed as grand as one of today's huge development houses. The house on Audubon Drive was a wood-frame board-and-batten style, with black shutters and a section of brick trimming the bedroom wing. Inside, it was spacious and pleasant, with wall-to-wall carpet and floral wallpaper and a white-brick fireplace.

It was a house far beyond Gladys's fantasies. The Presleys had lived in a public housing project and in small, run-down houses. And they had shared a bathroom with other tenants in tacky rooming houses. In Tupelo, they had rented tiny, nondescript houses without indoor plumbing. Now the days of struggle were over. They owned a decent house, at last – like other people had, a *new* house with private bedrooms and two lovely tiled bathrooms and no rats.

Now Gladys had twin state-of-the-art wall ovens. And Elvis bought her a new electric deep-fryer and two Mixmasters – so she could have one at each end of the counter and not have to walk so far. The family bought new furniture – a futuristic kind of Danish modern, special to the fifties. Always thrifty, Gladys stored all her old furniture in the spare bedroom (along with the overflow of fan mail), and she complained about how high-priced the curtains at Sears were. The house was too new to need redecorating – which was why Elvis's bedroom was pink and feminine. It would have been wasteful to change all the wallpaper and repaint everything. But slowly Elvis's parents began to indulge in a few luxuries. Gladys hung some wallpaper with musical motifs on it, and she placed decorative ceramics of musical figures on the wall. And then, while Elvis was away, she and Vernon converted part of the patio into a Florida room, with jalousie windows. That didn't last long. Elvis, moving into his new role as head of the family, had an even better idea. He ripped out the new wall and extended the room further towards the pool. He installed red carpeting, mahogany panelling, and a small turquoise-tiled bathroom. Then he turned the carport into a two-car garage and turned the detached garage into a pool house. His whimsical extravagance – now that he could afford it – was a pattern that would last the rest of his life.

The house on Audubon Drive was not ostentatious, or beyond the Presleys' means. Elvis's parents felt at home in it. At last they had enough space to move around in, with modern conveniences they had never had before. Elvis's grandmother Minnie Mae Presley, who had lived with them for years, could be comfortable there, and Elvis could have everything he needed. The financial pressures were lifting. They could enjoy themselves and invite over all their kinfolks and friends. Gladys had her garden. Her cornstalks leaned against some white-painted picketing. She grew purple-hull peas – long speckled pods of field peas that were brown when cooked. And in this new world they could have pets. The Presleys loved animals. They had dogs named Boyd and Sweetpea, a little spitz. And Elvis installed a pet monkey, Jayhew, in a gigantic cage, complete with trapeze.

Although the house was splendid, Gladys was not entirely at ease on Audubon Drive. She was used to visiting with her neighbours and keeping up with the news in her neighbourhood, as she did at Lauderdale Courts, the housing project. But here on Audubon Drive, neighbours kept to themselves and didn't necessarily have interests in common. Gladys felt isolated. She and Vernon didn't know what to do with themselves when Elvis was on the road, and they felt out of place in this upscale neighbourhood. Vernon puttered around. Gladys fretted that she couldn't keep chickens. She kept busy with scrapbooks. She and Minnie Mae watched TV.

Elvis's parents were accustomed to economizing. Gladys hung her wash outside – the sensible thing to do, to let the clothes dry in the sun rather than running expensive equipment. Vernon was even more frugal, and he practised his economies around the house, making rigged-up repairs. He saved every scrap. And then Elvis would come along and blow down a wall with some profligate new idea. 'Oh, Lordy,' Vernon would say.

The new house was a palace, at the outer limits of what Gladys and Vernon could comprehend and enjoy. But for Elvis, the sky was the limit: go wild, buy a Harley, get a monkey. The fans crowded into the carport to watch Elvis working on his motorcycle, or riding figure eights around the backyard and the adjacent lot. They dug up pieces of sod for souvenirs. They tried to pry bricks out of the lamp pillars. They stole the wash from the line.

At the end of the year, at Christmas, Elvis bought the grandest artificial Christmas tree he could find and heaped expensive presents beneath it.

JUNE IN JULY

ELVIS SEEMED TO have everything going for him that summer of 1956. Even though he had suffered from personal attacks on his character, he had fame, fortune, and freedom. He had given his parents the home that they deserved. And he had a girlfriend he wanted to marry – June Juanico. His summer idyll with June Juanico in Biloxi, Mississippi, was the best time of his life, he told her years later. This romance is recounted movingly, with reflection and humour and poignancy, in her memoir, *Elvis: In the Twilight of Memory*. The young Elvis she depicts comes to life as a sensitive, charming young man earnestly trying to create a genuine, normal life for himself with his newfound advantages. It is possibly the last glimpse we have of 'the real Elvis' – Elvis the young innocent – before the seductions of his career engulfed him like a tidal wave.

After he came home from New York, Elvis took his first real vacation in over a year. He had met June Juanico, a teenager from Biloxi, Mississippi, a year earlier, before he was nationally known. They spent the night together on the pier, talking and kissing and getting to know each other. They were eager to see each other again, but through miscommunication, they lost touch. One day in June 1956, June came to Memphis with her girlfriends, and they dared to drive out to Audubon Drive and take a look at Elvis's new house. June was embarrassed to be found bent over the white picket fence watching the bulldozer work on the swimming pool when Elvis drove up in the pink Cadillac with his parents. They had been to a funeral.

Between the time Elvis and June first met, in 1955, when he was a regional wonder with a local hit record, and the time they got together again, the world had spun around for Elvis, but he and June quickly took up where they had left off the year before. June was immediately accepted into the Presley household. Although Vernon rarely expressed himself, Gladys was ready for Elvis to get serious about a woman. June helped her shell purple-hull peas and cook, and she instructed June on how Elvis liked his chicken. She quizzed June on her home-making talents and her sewing. June had made her own skirt, and Gladys inspected 'the hem, the waistband, the zipper, even the kick-pleat in the back', June reported.

Elvis spent most of July with June in Biloxi. His exploits with women throughout his life are now legendary, and during his early days on the road, he reportedly had a different girl every night. But June Juanico holds a unique position among the women in his life because she was the last one he seemed to have a genuine relationship with before his superstardom took over. June was older and more sophisticated than Dixie, his first serious girlfriend. She was high-spirited, open and fun-loving, independent-minded and strong. She didn't fawn over Elvis because of his fame. She wasn't even a fan of his records. She thought he had such a beautiful voice he should be singing ballads like 'Over the Rainbow' rather than strange songs like 'Hound Dog'. She loved to sing, and they harmonized on tunes like 'Let the Rest of the World Go By' and 'Back in the Saddle Again'.

Elvis blew into Biloxi with several companions, guys he hung out with, and they rented a villa on a golf course until they got thrown out for shooting off fireworks. The summer was spent frolicking with June and her friends. Elvis didn't spend much money on her. They ate at diners and coffee shops – nothing fancier than cheeseburgers, except for po'boy sandwiches once in New Orleans. They didn't go shopping. He bought her few presents, no cars. (He got in the habit of bestowing cars on unsuspecting people later.) Even though the money was cascading into his bank account, Elvis was doing little splurging during July. High living was not familiar to him, and except for buying Cadillacs and motorcycles, he didn't exactly know what to do with his new wealth. His romance with June involved remarkably little of the big-star trappings and expensive toys he later indulged himself in. It seemed to exist on a normal level, in an actual place, not with pretensions or acquisitions. The clothes Elvis wore weren't the exaggerated costumes he wore in Memphis or on tour. Biloxi was sweltering; June was in shorts and sandals most of the time, and Elvis wore simple short-sleeved shirts and pants. They swam, water-skied, rode horses. Elvis got badly sunburned. They went skeet-shooting, aiming BB guns at 45-rpm records tossed from a stack on a broom handle. They spent evenings at a cocktail lounge. They drove to New Orleans. Elvis received his first gun, a shotgun, as a gift from June's mother's boyfriend – a thrill for a guy whose mother hadn't let him have a rifle and insisted on a guitar instead.

Elvis invited his parents to Biloxi. Vernon, still not accustomed to his freedom from having to scrounge for a living, was quiet. But he was fascinated by the roadside signs for tiny baby alligators and had to stop to investigate. June and Elvis took Vernon and Gladys deep-sea fishing. Gladys wore a pink dress and sunglasses. Even though she was seasick, she hooked a fifty-pound jackfish. She made Elvis peanut-butter-and-banana sandwiches and fed them to him while his hands were busy with his fishing gear. After the long day, when they were on land, she said, 'I feel like a newborn calf trying to find his legs.'

June Juanico remembers 'how sad but tender Mrs Presley's eyes were when she looked at her only child and feared for his safety. And how you could see in those eyes the hard times she had survived up until the time she didn't have to worry where the next meal was coming from. I think all this worry led to her looking much older than her years. On the other hand, Mr Presley, a man of few words or emotions, looked far younger, even with the gray hair.'

The day of the fishing trip was the day 'Don't Be Cruel' and 'Hound Dog' were released – a single record that sold four million copies by the end of the year. During that summer, 'Don't Be Cruel' and 'Hound Dog' dominated the airwaves, but June Juanico doesn't muddy her narrative with news of Elvis's career, paying scant attention to his new record or how he felt about it. With the pressures of his fame far away, Elvis reportedly relaxed and let himself fall in love. Among other intimacies, he shared with June his lifelong practice of staring at the moon until a blue ring appeared. 'Now, let yourself totally relax, and just focus on the space between the moon and the stars. Don't think about anything! Just let yourself float. If you can relax enough, you can go right up there with them.' He swore he was serious. 'People think you're crazy if you talk about things they don't understand,' he said. In turn, she gave him Kahlil Gibran's *The Prophet*, a book she cared deeply about. We know from other sources that Elvis was drawn into this book of meditations, read it many times, and kept it by his bedside for the rest of his life.

As June Juanico tells it, she and Elvis grew madly in love, and he asked her to marry him in three years. The Colonel (the man who had promised not to interfere with Elvis's private life) wouldn't let him get married yet because of his career. June hadn't met the Colonel, but already she disliked him.

During the summer, June began to notice the theatrical side of Elvis's personality, incongruous with his natural style of fun and humour. She saw black smudges under Elvis's eyes when he was in the pool, and he admitted it was mascara. The mascara was a foreshadowing, so to speak, of the artifice Elvis would rely on more and more in his effort to get away from the hard, crude realities he had grown up with. The summer idyll could not erase those ingrained memories.

And then, too soon, he returned to the life of Elvis the star. When he left for a twelve-day tour of Florida, he insisted that June and her friends accompany him. Until then, with June, the picture we have of Elvis is of someone so vibrant, sweet, and loving that we are under his spell. In Biloxi he was assured and relaxed and fun-loving and nice most of the time. His new fame had given him confidence and a sense of power. He had transcended his painful, awkward shyness. Elvis was comfortable with June and their friends in Biloxi, but back in the bigtime his old sense of shame and inadequacy returned; in dealing with the crowds around him backstage, he was still an outsider, self-conscious and uncertain. Only onstage did he seem free.

The Florida tour was a hurricane, a rough schedule of twelve days with two or three shows a day – a total of twenty-seven shows. Unable to bear the frenzy of the crowds, June and her friends skipped many of the shows and went shopping or to the beach. She stood back, not competing with the fans, but she could see what they saw – Elvis's utter beauty, his sexiness, his talent, his life force. The first moment she saw him over a year before, she knew he was the most gorgeous being she'd ever laid eyes on. But now June recoiled from the crowds, the inanity of the fans, the demands on Elvis's time and energy – the dangers his mother sensed.

June hated Colonel Parker, who seemed to control Elvis. Elvis seemed to give in to him. When word got out that Elvis was engaged, the Colonel forced him to deny it in public, insisting it would hurt his image. June said the Colonel was 'nothing more than a carny'. He even said 'Step right up, ladies and gentlemen' at his souvenir booths at the shows, she noted.

But if June had trouble with the crush of fans and the

pressures in Florida, it is also clear from her story that Elvis couldn't handle the storm either. He was maturing as an artist and wanting to improve his music, extend his range, experiment. He always wanted to please, but he wanted his own way, too, and he was racked by the criticisms that had continued to grow about his image. He especially hated the labels: Elvis the Pelvis, Sir Swivel Hips, the Hillbilly Cat. In a famous interview with *TV Guide*, done during the Florida tour, Elvis's temper flared in defence of his fans, who had been termed 'idiots' in a review. 'They're somebody's kids. They're somebody's decent kids, probably, that was raised in a decent home, and he hasn't got any right to call these kids idiots.' And he was angry when he had to defend his religion against the pejorative term 'Holy Roller' and its connotations of suggestive movements to spirited music. Elvis said, 'I always attended church where people sang, stood up and sang in the choir and worshiped God, you know. I have never used the expression "Holy Roller".'

'Was it peppy music?' the reporter demanded to know.

In Jacksonville, the county judge warned Elvis to tone down his act or face arrest. 'I can't figure out what I'm doing wrong,' Elvis said. 'I know my mother approves of it.' Refusing to relinquish his own control in Jacksonville, Elvis created the familiar hysteria by surprise moves – standing stock-still and quirking his index finger to mimic the Elvis gyration. June – in the wings – heard Elvis say 'Fuck you very much' while looking in the judge's direction in the audience. His voice did not carry above the wall of screams, but from her spot in the wings June could hear what he said.

'I guarantee they'll never do this to me again!' Elvis told

June later. 'If I ever come back to this fuckin' town, I hope they take me out back and shoot me.'

She had heard Elvis swear only occasionally, but now on the tour he swore continually. The pressures on Elvis upset her. He was surrounded by handlers, officials, bodyguards, press, record-label representatives, fans. It was hard to be with him in the way she was accustomed to. Increasingly, she had noticed, when he gathered more of his friends around, he was competitive and tried to be like them – tough and macho. And his possessiveness rankled her. When she saw some flashes of ugliness – his volatile temper, a quick, violent reflex – she knew it would be difficult for either of them to stay centred in the maelstrom to come.

After the frantic Florida fracas, June decided that the world of showbiz was not for her, and she suspected that with Elvis's impulsiveness and restlessness he wouldn't remain committed to her. Although she was even more deeply in love with him, she declined to come out to Hollywood when he invited her for the filming of his first movie, *Love Me Tender*, a black-and-white Civil War drama. But they talked on the telephone almost daily, and he confided in her about his feelings of intimidation in Hollywood. He said he felt he didn't belong there. He told her he dreamed he was running and jumping over tall buildings – like Superman – trying to get back to Biloxi.

June Juanico's story about the summer of 1956 reminds us of the Elvis we all want to remember – young and healthy and sexy, setting the world on fire; Elvis before he dyed his pretty light-brown hair so unnaturally black; Elvis before we knew any of the sad stories about his decline. We want to remember the polite, good-natured boy, saying 'Aw shucks, I never danced vulgar. I was just jiggling.'

Elvis could not give back the fame that had descended on him. He didn't really want to. And once he accepted that he was the King of Rock-and-Roll (*Variety* bestowed the title that year), then he could never trade it for being a nobody again.

TWISTER

IN SEPTEMBER 1956, Elvis returned to Tupelo with his parents. It was a far different journey from the one that had led them out of Tupelo in 1948. This time they weren't crammed into a jalopy with all their pots and pans. They drove a white Lincoln. It was Elvis Day, with a parade and fireworks in his honour. Elvis performed onstage at the Mississippi-Alabama Fair and Dairy Show, where he had first sung 'Ole Shep' at age ten.

His parents were dressed up, sipping bottled Cokes through straws, and clucking with pride. 'We had to miss the parade because we were eating dinner,' Gladys told a radio reporter. Vernon graciously thanked the city officials who arranged the special day. In this interview, he sounded so articulate and at ease that it is hard to picture the ne'er-do-well that Tupelo had once considered him. The big dudes who had once called the Presleys white trash were now rushing forward to claim Elvis.

He slammed onto the fairgrounds stage, twisted his hips, and writhed around wildly, mesmerizing a crowd of twenty thousand. He wore a sensational blue velvet shirt with full gathered sleeves and silver buttons – a heavy shirt not meant to be worn in the blazing heat of September in Mississippi. The girls squealed, and the city fathers strutted because a home-town boy had achieved national success. In spite of his notorious onstage behaviour, he made a good impression on the town's elite with his polite, humble manner offstage.

Elvis's appearance at the Tupelo fair was an extraordinary moment – for Tupelo, for Elvis, and for his parents. No accolade means quite as much as an accolade coming from one's home town. Gladys and Vernon could respond to that more readily than they could to praise coming from RCA executives in New York, for instance, or urgent telegrams from Hollywood. But Gladys said, 'It made me feel bad to go back there like that and remember how poor we was.' Vernon seemed happy, loosened up and in good humour, telling old acquaintances, 'The boy is taking good care of us.'

Gladys and Vernon were proud of their son's success, but in truth, Gladys felt deep confusion and sorrow. A thousand letters a week were arriving at Audubon Drive – half of them directed at her and Vernon for being bad parents, for raising such a hellion. Then, too, the fans crowding around the house night and day were becoming too much to handle. And the neighbours were complaining about the traffic and the noise – and the laundry on Gladys's wash line.

Gladys's health was poor. She was overstressed with worry about Elvis. He was home infrequently, and she was afraid her son would get hurt by crowds or corrupted by Hollywood. He was impulsive, extravagant, and even domineering in the way he had introduced so much unfathomable change into their lives. She longed for him to come home, marry June, and have children. She thought he should settle down and maybe run a little furniture business.

But Elvis was dancing in the middle of the whirlwind. He had been lionized, criticized, lambasted, rejected, rewarded, celebrated. The frenzy was accelerating. In early September he made his first national TV appearance since *The Steve Allen Show*. Ed Sullivan, once resistant to having him on his show, had caved in because of Elvis's immense popularity. He paid fifty thousand dollars to book Elvis for three appearances. This huge visibility zoomed Elvis into full national consciousness.

His first appearance on *The Ed Sullivan Show* came in September 1956. I remember watching with my parents and my little sister. We stood about two feet from the TV screen and stared, enthralled. Elvis, wearing a plaid jacket, sang 'Don't Be Cruel', 'Love Me Tender', 'Hound Dog', and 'Ready Teddy'. He wriggled and cavorted with such energy and good humour that we couldn't help but love him.

That month Elvis finished filming his first movie, *Love Me Tender*, in which he dies at the end. He was eager to prove himself as an actor, with wistful notions of becoming the next James Dean, the talented actor who had been killed not long before. Colonel Parker had a strategy to spirit Elvis away from the rock-and-roll controversy. By slinking Elvis into the movies, opening him up to a wider audience, he would get Elvis a more wholesome image and remove him from the threats of rock-and-roll, which after all was only a fad. And why waste him on television, where people could see him for free?

In Hollywood, Elvis fell in with a crowd of young actors, including Natalie Wood and Nick Adams, who boasted about his friendship with James Dean. Nick Adams, who was something of a hustler, came to visit in Memphis, and Gladys found him odd, with messy habits. When June Juanico came to spend a few days with the Presleys, she felt that Nick was an intrusion, and she didn't want to stay longer in order to meet Natalie Wood, who was coming in a few days. Elvis kept proclaiming it an innocent visit, but June didn't want to share him. She went home before Natalie arrived. Elvis showed Natalie the sights of Memphis. Natalie, accustomed to California luxury, was slumming when she cruised with Elvis on his motorcycle. They went riding on the Dodgem cars at the fairgrounds. And Elvis took her to WHBQ to meet Dewey Phillips. But Natalie was bored by Elvis's cheeseburger-and-roller-skating style of life. After a couple of days at Audubon Drive in a house overrun with peculiar country folks, she called home and pleaded for someone to get her out of there.

After Natalie's visit, Elvis's romance with June cooled. June wouldn't go to New York with him in October for the second *Ed Sullivan Show*. He had confided in June on the telephone almost every night while filming *Love Me Tender*, and he even sang the title song to her over the phone, but the fact was that Elvis had landed in Hollywood. Although he was intimidated by many of the people there and felt out of place at Hollywood parties, he also knew that many glamorous women were available. Elvis was never in his life a model of fidelity, except to his mother. The Colonel wanted Elvis to be seen with Hollywood stars for publicity purposes, but June blamed him for trying to manipulate Elvis's private life.

By the end of October, Elvis had sold ten million single records, two-thirds of RCA's output for the year. The Colonel made a three-picture contract and a merchandising deal to exploit everything from lunch boxes to pedal pushers with Elvis's name on them. The Colonel preferred to tantalize the public by rationing Elvis's recording sessions, keeping RCA hanging and not building a backlog. But clearly Elvis was happiest making music. He lingered over the process, aiming for the highest quality. Peter Guralnick wrote, 'Time meant nothing to him in the studio. If he felt like singing spirituals, he would sing spirituals to his heart's content. It was his way of finding his place; it was all part of the creative process as he had learned it in the Sun Studio. If the feeling wasn't there, you waited until it got there.' At a jam session in December at Sun Records with Jerry Lee Lewis, Carl Perkins, and Johnny Cash, Elvis displayed confidence, high spirits, and initiative. The group, sharing their heritage of gospel music, sang several songs they knew from church. At Elvis's suggestion, they sang 'Have a Little Talk with Jesus', and then Elvis turned it into a 'Hound Dog'-style rhythm-and-blues.

In December, *Love Me Tender* was released – a box-office smash and a critical dud. But now Elvis was a millionaire. He bought more Cadillacs and an old truck. When he performed in Louisville, he visited his long-lost grandfather, Jessie Presley, and bought him a Ford Fairlane. The Louisville police filmed Elvis's concert, just in case he did anything obscene. He was made an honorary colonel by the Louisiana governor, theoretically placing him equal in rank to Colonel Parker. At Christmas, Elvis had a Las Vegas showgirl visiting at his house. When June read this in the newspaper, she knew she had lost him.

The pace didn't let up in 1957. On his third Sullivan appearance, he wore the blue velvet shirt, with a gold lamé vest. For this final Sullivan appearance, because of the unrelenting charges of vulgarity and lewdness, Elvis was televised from the waist up only. He sang 'Don't Be Cruel' with the Jordanaires, a rhythmic performance – influenced by Jackie Wilson's interpretation of the song – that makes clear the gospel roots of rock-and-roll. Then he sang 'Peace in the Valley', written by the black gospel composer Thomas A. Dorsey and popularized by country singer Red Foley. After the song, Ed Sullivan, the man who had once declared he wouldn't touch Elvis with a ten-foot pole, told the audience, 'This is a real decent, fine boy,' and he said to Elvis, 'We want to say that we've never had a pleasanter experience on our show with a big name than we've had with you.'

Early in the year, Elvis made another movie, *Loving You*, in which his light-brown hair was dyed black – an effect he liked because he thought it accented his features. Gladys and Vernon took a train to Hollywood with their new friends, the pool contractor and the house painter who had worked on their house on Audubon Drive. (The neighbours there may have been aloof, but the workmen were more the Presleys' sort.) In Hollywood, they visited Elvis on the set and ended up appearing in the film as extras, Gladys applauding like his best fan as he performs a song. *Loving You* is the prototype of the Elvis movie. Most Elvis movies would turn out to be variations of the Story of Elvis, not brooding, complex, James Dean-like rebel films. *Loving You* is perhaps the most authentic of them, for in it Elvis still has his fresh appeal and innocent zest. It is the story of Deke Rivers, a lonely orphan with a singing talent and an insidious manager who asks him to sign a fifty-fifty contract. (The story was strangely close to Elvis's actual situation with Colonel Parker. It is unclear why Parker allowed such a plot, since he tried to keep Elvis ignorant of business dealings.) Elvis's performances of 'Loving You', a Leiber and Stoller ballad, and 'Gotta Lotta Livin' to Do' are the essence of the early Elvis, filmed with a good sampling of leg manoeuvres and jiggling, and the movie, although fairly shallow, captures Elvis's personality and talent credibly. The movie's narrative is a simplified version of the moral complexities that faced Elvis in real life – the conflict between his soul and his fame.

In the new world of opportunity that had opened up to him, Elvis was on uncertain footing. He was tense and jittery, and he tended to get in fights. In March, Elvis sent a telegram to June Juanico, asking her to meet his Los Angeles-to-Memphis train during its stopover in New Orleans. He hadn't called her since 26 December. He said he had a surprise for her. She drove over from Biloxi and informed him she was engaged to be married. Elvis had expected her to take him back, even though he hadn't been faithful to her. He was stunned. In their brief meeting, he didn't mention the surprise he had for her. Apparently, his disappointment was genuine and long-lasting, although he said little about it directly. The next day, June saw in the paper the news about Elvis's purchase of Graceland, a mansion on the outskirts of Memphis.

Gladys and Vernon had found Graceland themselves. It was out in the country, sitting on thirteen acres, where Gladys could have some chickens at last. And Gladys, her health deteriorating, needed a restful place. The mansion, built in 1939 of Tishomingo limestone with white columns, was set off from the road, and it had a fence. The Audubon Drive house, comfortable as it was, had become impossible to live in. Even though they had erected a low wrought-iron fence, with two strands of barbed wire, Elvis's parents could not cope with the steady stream of strangers. Fans sometimes knocked on the door in the middle of the night. The neighbours, unhappy about the crowds and the noise (not just motorcycles – a helicopter once dropped Elvis off in the vacant lot next to his house), had got up a petition to try to buy the Presleys' house from them. Elvis was furious. His fans were responsible for his success and he wouldn't hear of snubbing them. The neighbours backed off when they learned Elvis's house was the only house on the block that was paid for.

During the week in Memphis when he bought Graceland, Elvis got into one of many altercations that would characterize his life. A marine accused Elvis of pulling a gun on him, claiming Elvis had insulted his wife. It was a prop gun from Hollywood that Elvis had been showing people. Troubled by the bad publicity the event generated – and, probably, genuinely embarrassed by his own conduct – Elvis wrote a rambling telegram to the private. He tried to explain the need he felt to be constantly on guard. Elvis wrote, 'I got a lucky break in life and I am very thankful for it but there are a few people who want to take shots at me. The majority of the people all over the world are very nice but there are a few who want to prove something. I have talked my way out of trouble so many times that I couldn't even count them not because I was afraid but just because I was always the type of person that never did believe in fighting and all that kind of stuff unless I thought it was absolutely necessary.'

Yet Elvis found himself in fights. He had inherited a hair-trigger temper from his mother. And he also got it from his culture, where resentment smouldered underneath the polite-ness to one's superiors. Elvis never fully overcame that sense of inferiority so deeply ingrained in him. He depended on others to protect him. One of his bodyguard pals, Red West, protected Elvis so fiercely that he kept getting in trouble himself.

The pitfalls of celebrity increasingly overshadowed Elvis. After an eight-city concert tour was marred by riots and protests, Elvis came home to Audubon Drive. On Easter Sunday, soon after his break-up with June, he told a minister, 'I am the most miserable young man you have ever seen. I have got more money than I can ever spend. I have thousands of fans out there, and I have a lot of people who call them-selves my friends, but I am miserable.' Elvis's new single, 'All Shook Up', was number one.

Amid the hubbub, the Presleys were preparing to move into their mansion – another improbable turn in their lives. Renovations were under way, and Elvis had installed the now-famous gates with the guitar and the musical notes. Elvis was photographed against the gates, in a *film noir* sort of picture in which the wrought iron casts shadow bars onto his jacket. He is staring pensively at the gates, as if wondering whether Graceland was going to be a prison for him.

And there was something more foreboding looming over him. The most famous young man in the world, trying to juggle his golden opportunities, expected to be drafted into the Army. He had already undergone his compulsory pre-induction physical exam. He feared that if he was whisked off into the Army for two years, his career would come to a crashing end.

Before long, he began filming *Jailhouse Rock*, another Story of Elvis movie. In this one, Elvis begins his rocking career while in prison, then rises to the top upon release. It was a whopping success financially but a critical disaster. Elvis was shaken, his gloom deepened by the accidental death of his co-star, Judy Tyler, soon after the filming was completed. He wouldn't ever go see the movie. Adding to his trouble was the estrangement of his musicians and pals Scotty and Bill. After they appeared with Elvis in *Jailhouse Rock*, Scotty and Bill were phased out of Elvis's career. Although they had been essential to developing Elvis's style and sound, neither the Colonel nor RCA could see the need for them when studio musicians could be hired. Elvis had told Scotty and Bill he would pay them more, but he lacked the courage to face the Colonel over the issue. Elvis, who had no idea how to manage business matters, was not even equipped to discharge the personal obligations of his own ambitions. He floundered, he goofed off, he hid. He went out with a Las Vegas exotic dancer named Tempest Storm, dated a female wrestler, toured less.

It would be hard to separate the various influences that descended on Elvis in the crazed beginning of his career, when every opportunity came his way and every teenage fantasy seemed to materialize. He was swept up in one of the most fabulous success rides anybody has ever had. He was raking in the money. The Colonel was getting him deals unheard of in Hollywood. Elvis was surrounding himself with new friends. The group of guys he would rely on as a buffer zone for the rest of his life was taking shape.

Elvis occasionally tried to step back and ground himself in reality. Usually, that meant going home, but now Elvis hardly saw his parents because he was away so much. He didn't see how sad his mother was; she was so overjoyed when he came home that he probably gave little thought to the strain she lived under while he was away, even though they talked on the telephone constantly. He didn't seem to be in love again right away. And he probably didn't know himself what he really felt. In early January of 1957, when he came home from New York after being on *The Ed Sullivan Show*, he went to see his old girlfriend Dixie Locke. From time to time he checked back with her, as if to get his bearings. Now Dixie was married, but he still had to touch base.

Elvis was caught in the funnel of the storm. It was tossing him around and around. On days when he didn't claim to be the most miserable young man in the world, he might have said he was the luckiest guy in the world. But at the end of 1957, he was drafted into the Army, and he thought his life was over.

GLADYS

WHEN ELVIS WAS inducted into the Army, the Colonel staged a media send-off. He was promoting Elvis as a patriotic, good boy, doing his duty. For Gladys, the Army held even more terrors than the loose life of Hollywood. She and Vernon accompanied Elvis to the induction centre on the unhappy day, sending their son off to boot camp at Fort Chaffee, Arkansas. Gladys wore a black velvet dress with a little dip in the neckline exposing a piece of white lace. It was the sort of dress one might wear to the theatre or a formal party – or a funeral. The induction was at 6:35 a.m., 24 March, 1958. In the pictures, Gladys's face is puffy from crying, the black circles under her eyes prominent.

After basic training, when Elvis was settled at Fort Hood, Texas, he found a three-bedroom trailer home so that his parents could join him. He could live off base if he had dependents. Later, after Memphis buddy Lamar Fike moved in with them as bodyguard, they rented a larger house, and then Elvis's cousins Gene and Junior Smith joined the group. Gladys willingly left Graceland behind, but she did not want to go to Germany, Elvis's next assignment. All Gladys knew was that the Germans had been the enemy in the war, and she was afraid if her boy went there he might have to go to a new war. 'I just can't see myself over there in a foreign country,' she told Lamar. 'I've left nothing over there, and I'm not trying to find anything.'

All that summer in Texas, Gladys was feeling 'poorly'. She returned to Memphis to see her own doctor, and when she was hospitalized Elvis almost went AWOL in his desperation to reach her bedside. He got to Memphis only a short time before she died, apparently of a heart attack, on 14 August, 1958.

In a photograph from that week, Elvis and his father are sitting side by side on the steps of Graceland. Elvis's arm rests on his father's back, and Vernon is embracing his son. Elvis has on a white short-sleeved shirt with vertical ruffles down the front. Their heads are bowed in tears. Someone heard Vernon say – maybe here, maybe a while before, or a while later – 'Elvis, look at them chickens. Mama ain't never gonna feed them chickens no more.'

'No, Daddy, Mama won't never feed them chickens any more.'

It was like a gospel call and response, this expression of grief that gained release through reiteration. The death of Elvis's mother was unexpected, and it was imponderable. For a young man such as Elvis, so attached to his parents, so bent on lifting his parents out of the misery of their lives, this loss was devastating. Elvis was inconsolable, his grief near hysteria.

Elvis and Gladys had doted on each other. Sometimes

when he came home to the house on Audubon Drive he lifted his mother by the waist and whirled her around in the driveway. They had always talked baby talk to each other, using pet names. They loved each other in a way that by modern standards might seem almost pathological but that was actually commonplace in the past. Their hardships had brought them close together – their visits to the prison when Elvis was a tot, the moving from one doomed little rat-trap house to another. It seemed to shock interviewers that he lived with his parents, as well as assorted other relatives. But kinship loyalty in the South demanded that kind of interlocking responsibility.

'My mama loved beautiful things, but she wouldn't wear them,' Elvis lamented when he gazed upon the baby-blue dress his mother was wearing in her silver casket. Of course she wouldn't wear fancy clothes around the house. Pretty things were too good to wear – why wear a nice dress to the dinner table and spill something on it? Only high-class people could afford to waste things and were indifferent to the work that went into keeping good clothes presentable.

Gladys had commented many times that she wished they could go back to being poor. The new luxuries could not compensate for Elvis's absences and the dangers she saw threatening him – crazed fans, irate parents, Hollywood thugs. She pined for him. She worried. She drank and gained weight. She had bad nerves. And she had chronic hepatitis. Even though she felt unwell, she wouldn't seek adequate medical care.

Her mother, Doll Smith, had been an invalid, with tuberculosis. Even before she became tubercular, she had had languid spells, long periods in which she was bedridden from lassitude and needed to be waited on. At Graceland, Gladys – who had had some spells like that in high school – retreated from the world. She was depressed and worn out. She wore her simple handmade housedresses and eventually just went around in her housecoat. She grew some vegetables and turnip greens. She liked to pick Elvis a 'mess of greens'. She got pleasure out of Vernon's hogs and her chickens. The place was a menagerie – four donkeys, an attack turkey called Bowtie, two monkeys, assorted dogs. On one occasion Elvis and Vernon and bodyguard Lamar Fike drove to a farm to fetch some fowl for Gladys for a surprise. They hauled twenty chickens, eight ducks, six guineas, and a turkey home in the back seat of Elvis's yellow Fleetwood Cadillac, which was fouled almost beyond recovery.

June Juanico visited Elvis at Graceland when she came to Memphis with her bowling team a few years after her marriage and after Gladys's death. It was June's first sight of the mansion. She wrote, 'I was happy for Elvis, but at the same time I was heartbroken; not for myself, but for his mother. The mansion was so much like the ante-bellum homes she had admired on the Gulf Coast of Mississippi. I could still picture her oohing and ahing, trying to get Vernon to share her enthusiasm.'

But Gladys, even though she had chosen Graceland out of necessity, couldn't really feature herself as a mistress of a mansion. She was not happy at Graceland. It was too big for a home. She lived in the kitchen. Sounding remarkably like her son, she told a cousin, 'I'm miserable. I'm guarded. I can't go buy my own groceries. I can't go to the movies. I can't see my neighbors. I'm the most miserable woman in the world.' She'd stare out the window and dip snuff. Gladys usually drank Schlitz beer, concealed Southern-style in a paper sack. Elvis disapproved – too many family members were drunks and had come to bad ends. He was so determined to escape such a fate that he rarely drank himself.

There is some film footage of Gladys and Vernon walking out to the pink Cadillac, which is parked in front of Graceland on a winter's day. They play with the snow, a rare treat in a Southern clime. Vernon gives her a snowball to eat, playing and teasing, and she tosses a snowball towards the camera. She's in her thin dress and wool coat and pumps and a head scarf. They get into the Cadillac and drive down the driveway, and then they return, a lively boxer dog greeting the car.

It is a glimpse into their new life, but they seem essentially unchanged, as you can tell by Vernon's playfulness, and by the way Gladys walks and what she wears. Gladys seems frumpy, dispirited – she tries to clown for the camera, but her motions are tentative, half-hearted. She scoops up a little snow and, without packing it, tosses it languidly towards the photographer.

She lived at Graceland for a little over a year. Vernon's brother Vester and her brother Travis and some cousins manned the gates, so in a sense life was more manageable than it had been at Audubon Drive. Still, there were so many people around. The house was full. Servants – they had servants! Gladys huddled with her little spitz, Sweetpea, kissing and hugging him. She had dark circles under her eyes. She hung her wash out on the line and tended her garden. A country woman with a long history of making do, Gladys was plain-spoken, strong-willed, and expressive, yet soft-hearted and loving. But she still hated Colonel Parker for, among other things, trying to tell her how to dress and act in order to create an image of a little church-going lady.

Her nervousness is often attributed to the trauma of losing Elvis's twin at birth. And it is perfectly plausible that the deep pain Elvis himself suffered all his life originated with the death of Jesse Garon. His attachment to his mother reasonably flows from that, as if Elvis had to be both children – for his mother and for himself. The loss of his twin suffused his life experience, and certainly Gladys spoke frequently about Jesse Garon. Elvis was preoccupied throughout his life with questions about his twin.

If the loss of his twin at birth set the tone for Elvis's childhood, then one could say that the loss of his mother set the tone for the rest of his life. Elvis specialists often remark that he lost his moral compass after Gladys died. Many years later, when he felt he had lost his way, he confided to a woman in Hollywood that his mother would have known what to do. Elvis always said, 'Mama raised me right.'

Elvis's grief was so intense that he found it difficult to let his mother's body go. He kept touching her and talking to her, crying inconsolably. Sam Phillips sat up with him through the night, and others arrived to join the vigil over Gladys's body.

Elvis asked the Blackwood Brothers, Gladys's favourite gospel quartet, to sing at her funeral. He and Vernon almost collapsed during the service, and when she was buried, Elvis cried, 'Everything I have is gone.'

Once again, Elvis called on Dixie Locke for comfort. She came to the funeral, and he asked her to come to Graceland later. When they visited together, reminiscing about Gladys, he told Dixie he would like to give up his career. He was despondent. Nothing seemed to make sense to him. But he also vacillated and, perhaps, rationalized. He said he wanted to quit, but he couldn't. 'There are too many people that depend on me,' he told her. 'I'm in too far to get out.'

Gladys had taught Elvis politeness; she had instilled her own fearfulness in him. In teaching him subservience, she had held Elvis back in various ways, and his explosive energy on the stage may have resulted in part from the bursting of these restraints. Gladys had worried herself sick over him. She looked older than she was. In many photographs she looks frightened – or passive, resigned to the tumult around her.

As Elvis became more confident of his success, he had grown more resistant to her apron strings. She and Elvis argued and had fights – precisely because she was overly protective. But he was still the good son, the boy who telephoned home every night when he was on the road. He dismissed her worries and went on his energetic way. His sorrow after her death may have been deepened by a sense of failure. In his desire to lift his family out of poverty, he had helped to create a set of circumstances that made Gladys wish they were poor again. He hadn't given his parents what would have made them happiest. Jewels, cars, and kitchen appliances weren't enough. The thrills of a mansion and a few Cadillacs had their limits. Basically, Gladys and Vernon felt out of place, and Gladys was troubled and sick. So Elvis must have believed he failed his mother. Perhaps she should have had better medical care, earlier. Elvis had found himself the breadwinner and the man in charge, but he was too immature to have a grasp of his responsibilities in the midst of all the pressures on him.

Before his Army bereavement leave was up, Elvis went to the roller rink after hours and skated for hours by himself. He had been in the habit of renting the rink for parties, but now he had to be alone.

When he was a child, Gladys had discouraged Elvis from playing rough games. After she died, Elvis increasingly played violent games and roughhoused with his bodyguard pals. They played football and formed dangerous crack-the-whip lines at the roller rink. Elvis eventually learned karate, and he collected guns and carried them on his person everywhere he went.

Gladys's death liberated Elvis, but it was an equivocal liberation. He had lived an odd double life, rebel rocker and mama's boy, strutting sexual icon and polite, diffident son. He was building a history of women leaving him, and now after losing his mother he was to enter a strange new phase of his life. Without her moral authority, there would be no restraints on his life from now on out.

GERMANY

THERE'S A PHOTOGRAPH of Elvis, in his Army uniform, having breakfast with his father at a small kitchen table. His grandmother, Minnie Mae Presley, is standing between them with a plate of biscuits. Vernon and Elvis rest their arms on the table, working-class style, anchoring themselves in front of their plates. On the wall is a cross-stitched sampler, and in the background is a box of Premium Saltines. On the table is a carton of milk. Minnie Mae's plate is empty. By custom, she is serving the men first.

This scene could be in Memphis. But it is in Germany, where Elvis's father and his grandmother came to live with him while he finished his Army duty. They rented a three-storey, five-bedroom white stucco house in Bad Nauheim.

They're in Germany, but the characters in the picture have brought Memphis with them. On the table, near the milk carton, is a tin of McCormick's black pepper. Like many Southerners, Elvis topped his plate of food with a thick layer of pepper. The pepper tin on the table was a familiar sight in the South. The pepper was never transferred to a pepper shaker but remained in its homely package because it had more holes – perfect for crop-dusting the plate.

Elvis, far from home, had to surround himself with the familiar. He knew what he liked. He liked his eggs cooked hard and his bacon burned. And he wanted his family with him. But how sad this photo is: Vernon and Elvis, off in a foreign land, without Gladys. The looks in their eyes are desolate. Vernon seems wary and uncomfortable, Elvis a bit hardened. Minnie Mae's head dips modestly – in that manner of very tall people (she was as tall as Elvis and skinny as a pole), and she manages a small smile for the camera. Elvis was devoted to his grandmother, whom he called Dodger. She was a strong woman, who dipped a little snuff, bopped people over the head with a skillet, and cussed with a lively tongue. She spoiled Elvis. But she would slap him when he played tricks on her.

Even though Elvis's grandmother had brought her Mississippi culture to Germany and was trying her best to hold the family together, Elvis's overseas experience had a tinge of the weird. It was an unusual household. Besides his father and his grandmother, Elvis housed Memphis buddies Red West and Lamar Fike, who had been with him for some time, for companionship and security. Elvis increasingly needed a lot of people around him. With these guys, Elvis spent his free time acting like a kid – playing pranks, rough-housing, playing violent games of football in the park with a bunch of tough German guys. Now Gladys was not around to stop him, and Minnie Mae was not such a worry-wart.

Those seventeen months were a strange hiatus. Elvis was suspended between worlds. He spent his days as a reluctant dogface, an ordinary GI. Then in the evenings, he returned to the family's little Memphis-on-the-Rhine. He was Elvis the singing star, and he wasn't. He was a soldier, and he wasn't. He had never wanted to go. Although he was not suited to the Army, reports of his behaviour as a soldier are admiring and complimentary, especially praising his humility and his desire to be treated like a regular person. He excelled in tank training and was routinely promoted to specialist fourth class. But he was homesick and depressed. He longed for Reese's peanut butter cups and asked a friend to send him some. He kept up with all the latest music, especially anything by Roy Orbison. He telephoned to America frequently. He spent hours on the phone with Anita Wood, his latest girlfriend, a Memphis entertainer. He wrote her about getting married and having a 'little Elvis'. Two weeks later, he was dating a woman who resembled Brigitte Bardot.

Colonel Parker had kept Elvis out of Special Services, which would have used his talents as an entertainer, and urged him into regular military duty to show his patriotism and to foster an all-American image. But Elvis hated the Army. He was stricken by the fear that by the time he got out, his career would be over. Colonel Parker, always pragmatic, had taken measures to maintain Elvis's career while he was away by occasionally releasing singles that Elvis had already recorded. The Colonel cleverly timed the record releases so that a hunger for Elvis's return would build. And he arranged for a steady stream of Elvis merchandise to flow into the teen market. He even sold Elvis dogtags.

Elvis was worried that new musical stars would emerge to

replace him, and he would be forgotten. The Colonel wrote him chatty, cheerful letters almost every day, trying to keep Elvis's spirits up, but also making sure he had Elvis under his thumb. By long distance, the Colonel orchestrated events in Germany, such as a tea with four German teenagers who had won a contest. Anita Wood had her passport and was all set to go to Germany to visit Elvis, but the Colonel wouldn't allow her to go – it would pose an image problem. At home, he instigated an Elvis Presley Midget Fan Club.

While the singles were selling millions back home, the Colonel wouldn't let Elvis give any performances while he was in the Army. He didn't want Elvis to perform for free. Elvis wasn't even allowed to sing at the talent show on the troop ship carrying him overseas. He couldn't sing in shows on the base or accept invitations anywhere else to perform. The ban increased Elvis's worry that his career was over.

But music – and possible career moves – were constantly on his mind. He sang all the time in private, with friends. He thought about the music he wanted to record, he experimented, he listened. He wanted to do grander, more soulful songs. He rented a piano and recorded some songs with Charlie Hodge, one of his Army pals who later became part of his entourage and a guitarist in his band. The Colonel had suggested that Elvis make some home tapes, with just his voice and the piano. On a tape recorder Vernon got him for Christmas, Elvis recorded some gospel numbers, and he recorded 'Oh, Lonesome Me', 'Are You Lonesome Tonight?', 'Danny Boy', 'Soldier Boy', 'The Fool', 'I'm Beginning to Forget You', and 'There's No Tomorrow'. The titles alone seem to tell a story of Elvis's state of mind.

Although it was a period of some musical growth for Elvis, mostly his time in Germany was a corrupting interlude, a period of disintegration. Elvis began the self-destructive patterns of behaviour he would follow for the rest of his life. When he got leave, he and his Memphis pals went out tomcatting in Paris and Munich. They headed for the striptease clubs. They entertained whole chorus lines in their hotel. They had shaving-cream fights and water fights, set off fireworks in hotels, wrecked cars. In the rented house in Bad Nauheim, Elvis had a stream of girlfriends slipping up to his bedroom. But he wasn't happy in Germany. Long stretches of dull Army routine alternated with adolescent binges, and the result was restless emptiness.

His father was no help. Barely three months after Gladys died, Vernon began an affair with an Army officer's wife. Elvis was enraged and hurt by what he considered the dishonour to his mother's memory. (Vernon eventually married Dee Stanley, but Elvis never truly accepted the marriage, even though he was kind to her three boys.) Then, on the heels of his father's indiscretion, Elvis fell in love with an under-age girl.

Priscilla Beaulieu was an Army officer's stepdaughter. She was only fourteen, ten years younger than Elvis, and she appeared sweet and fragile in her sailor dress and bobby sox. Before she moved with her family from Texas to Germany, Priscilla had been aware that Elvis was stationed there, and she was determined to meet him. She has told her story in *Elvis and Me*: how Elvis, after hearing about her, had her fetched to his house – his large, crowded household – and then took her to his bedroom, promising not to hurt her;

and how she kept returning to visit, for six months, until Elvis left Germany. She wrote, 'I saw him as he really was after he lost his mother. He shared his grief with me, he was very insecure, and he felt betrayed by his father. ... He was at his most vulnerable, his most honest, I would say his most passionate during that time.'

We are left to speculate and imagine that Elvis, still grieving for his mother and disappointed in love, set out to mould the girl of his dreams by choosing one too young to challenge him. Although she spent evenings with Elvis in his bedroom, Priscilla insists that their relationship was not consummated until their wedding night, almost eight years later. Priscilla was undeniably beautiful. Her face was classically angelic, her figure petite yet full. She must have seemed both sweet and sexy. And her youth and innocence must have been great attractions to a young man who was in so many ways still a boy.

The Army itself was supposed to make a man of him, and it did so, but in an illusory way. In the Army, he was introduced to drugs – by his superiors. It seemed innocent. Amphetamines – speed – were popular ways of losing weight, staying awake, borrowing extra energy. For Elvis, who had essentially a hyperactive personality – jittery and charged with sexual energy – speed heightened his natural exuberance and banished his depression, enabling him to accomplish his duties and giving him endurance for night-time tank patrols. Elvis loved the pills and believed they could not be harmful, since prescription pills were legal. How could they be harmful, if guys in the US Army had them, and if they made you feel so terrific? Elvis had to bolster himself with whatever props he could find – he doctored his spirit with pills the same as he doctored his food with black pepper. For the rest of his life, he would be a night person, and he would use speed to keep going. The pills gave him physical strength, and more important, a kind of false moral courage.

A boy at heart, Elvis had to be the man of a huge extended family – his relatives, his friends, his growing entourage, his fans. He had major financial and artistic obligations – he had to assert an authority he did not feel entitled to. The pills were his way of commanding authority.

Elvis went to Germany naive and innocent and returned with a darker, more worldly soul. It is an ironic twist, because at the beginning of his career Elvis had an image as a dangerous, sexually threatening rebel, when actually he was a sweet boy devoted to his mother and eager to please. But when Elvis returned from the Army, the Colonel's aim was to erase Elvis's rock-and-roll rebel image and turn him into a mainstream all-American boy next door, safe for America. He was to be the clean-cut GI, returning in pure-hearted triumph.

The Colonel orchestrated Elvis's return, with press conferences, whistle stops, receptions, and a new single release called 'Stuck on You', which quickly reached number one. The Colonel persuaded Senator Estes Kefauver to read a tribute to Elvis into the *Congressional Record*. Elvis landed on Frank Sinatra's TV show, performing a duet with Sinatra of 'Witchcraft', and ending with 'Love Me Tender'. Elvis was controlled, cool, restrained. Peter Guralnick described 'a new Elvis, a modified Elvis, who suggests motion without precipitating it, who elicits genuine screams by indirection rather than assault'. It was a triumphant return for Elvis, who feared Sinatra would make fun of him, the way Steve Allen had. Frank Sinatra had once said rock-and-roll was music for 'cretinous goons'. But now the Chairman of the Board was all smiles.

A LONELY TEENAGER

WHEN ELVIS RETURNED from Germany in 1960, his hair was its natural sandy colour, and he had lost the baby fat in his face. People noticed his new air of worldliness.

Eager to resume his career, he recorded an album, *Elvis Is Back*, and later in the year a gospel album, both of which fully engaged his artistry. He recorded 'Fever' and 'Are You Lonesome Tonight?' and Lowell Fulsom's R&B hit 'Reconsider Baby'. Elvis's next number-one hit single was 'It's Now or Never', his arrangement of the Enrico Caruso standard 'O sole mio', which Gladys had once played for Elvis on the Victrolla. With this song, Elvis had a chance to project his voice into a richer, more complex kind of music. It was what he had been building up to during his Army hiatus. Now he plunged into working on his craft.

But he was eager to develop his acting talent too. The Colonel, who had steered Elvis through the rock-and-roll frenzy on his way to the top, now manoeuvred him through the Hollywood shoals, making deals so far in advance that Elvis was locked into filming schedules for years to come.

Elvis accepted the Colonel's guidance. He became bigger than ever, his wholesome celluloid image defusing the controversies of the pre-Army period. Elvis made a string of highly lucrative movies, with accompanying soundtrack albums that were also highly profitable – such as *GI Blues*, *Blue Hawaii*, and *Fun in Acapulco*. The Colonel shaped Elvis's career so that by the mid-sixties, Elvis was one of the top box-office stars with some of the best movie deals.

Elvis's fears had been unfounded; far from being over, his career flourished. But at a deeper level, the Colonel's manipulations proved disastrous. Elvis stopped touring and spent a large amount of his studio time in the sixties on soundtrack recordings of questionable quality. They were recorded under mechanical, businesslike conditions, with regulation union breaks – conditions that shattered Elvis's focus and inspiration. Elvis's creativity suffered from lack of challenge, and he found himself increasingly frustrated. He knew his films were mediocre, and he was embarrassed by many of the songs he was asked to record. But he clung to the hope that he would be offered better material – in both movies and music.

Meanwhile, during the early sixties, Elvis settled into a way of life designed to accommodate his fame and to compensate for his frustrations. He had been traumatized by the loss of his mother and by the Army's intrusion into his career. How was he supposed to behave now, when he could make the rules, when his mother was dead and his father so ineffectual? Elvis took charge of his own amusement and comfort, leaving his career up to the Colonel and his personal finances up to his penny-pinching father. Elvis had no idea what anything cost. Spending money wildly, indulging all his fancies, became, for him, an expression of freedom.

He hated Hollywood and deliberately kept his ties to Memphis. Graceland was his home; the luxurious places he rented in California were impersonal, not homes he cherished. He never felt confident enough to mingle with sophisticated people, so he stayed with his own group. His cousin Billy Smith said, 'Elvis wanted friends who were in touch with that Southern world that he came from, not actors and producers from the Hollywood scene. He wanted this little group that talked the same way he did and ate the same kind of food.' But Elvis, always wanting acceptance, was conscious of the poor image Southerners had. He worked to get rid of his accent.

Gradually Elvis assembled his group of loyal buddies – including cousins and high school classmates – who protected him and handled the logistics of being Elvis, everything from scheduling to transportation to ordering pizza. After they showed up in dark suits in Las Vegas, hovering around Elvis, they became known as the Memphis Mafia. This circle was composed of muscle men and amusing personalities who would do anything to be with Elvis. This kind of loyalty was possible because Elvis's charisma was so powerful. Orbiting him, his satellites felt significant.

Being with Elvis was undeniably fun. He had a huge sense of humour. He loved football, karate, riding horses, entertaining people, singing, and telling stories. He loved wordplay – he could never resist turning words on themselves. 'Heartbreak Hotel' became 'Heartburn Motel'. He called *Rebel Without a Cause* 'Rebel Without a Pebble'.

The guys loved Elvis for his quirks and for the thrill of being present at his all-night jam sessions and adventures. There were always clouds of pretty women floating around – women for Elvis and women for his friends. And with Elvis, anything might happen. In the later years, he might decide on a moment's notice to go to Las Vegas and stay in his penthouse suite or fly to Houston to buy an aeroplane. And they would all tag along. Life with Elvis was a movable party.

For years, the camaraderie was silly horseplay. When Elvis and his guys played touch football, there was a knock-down, drag-out, free-for-all style to their merriment. In the fifties, when they began going to California for the film productions, they got thrown out of hotels in Hollywood for having water fights in the halls. A three-hour pie fight at the Beverly Wilshire in the pre-Army days set the standard. At Graceland on the Fourth of July, Elvis and his pals engaged in reckless Roman-candle wars, throwing lighted fireworks at each other.

Elvis habitually rented the Memphis fairgrounds after midnight for hours of play on the Dodgem bumper cars and the Pippin (the roller coaster) with his friends and entourage. Always testing the limits, Elvis might ride the roller coaster seventeen times in a row. He rented the Memphian Theatre after hours for private showings. Thirty people might go along with him to watch whatever Elvis wanted to watch. They loaded up on hot dogs and popcorn – the works, courtesy of Elvis. Sometimes he would watch only the first reel and reject it and request another movie. Sometimes he'd watch the same movie over and over – *Dr Strangelove* four times in a row. The thirty guests and members of the entourage would have to sit there all night, trying to stay awake, aware that they were in the room with *Elvis*!

Throughout the sixties, Elvis was living out a teenage boy's fantasy. Rock-and-roll music itself twisted the physical energy of labour into joy and sexuality. Elvis was liberated from work; he could play and sing anything he desired; he could stay up all night, in defiance of the necessity his forebears had always faced of rising to toil in the sun. Music, not the drudgery of working, was the life force. Elvis was not going to toil, picking cotton or driving a mule. And he'd be damned if he'd wear dirty work clothes. He was free from nature.

Elvis loved driving. Motor vehicles could always take him to somewhere better. A Cadillac limousine replaced the mule team. He had learned to drive when he was ten, and his parents were letting him drive their truck on the highway by the time he was twelve. 'All I wanted to do was drive a truck,' Elvis once said. Dreaming of escape, he and his cousin Gene Smith as children had played beneath the porch, fashioning little race-car tracks in the dirt for their handmade toy cars (spools and rubber bands). Elvis found meaning in the vehicles he began to accumulate as soon as he had money. He loved motorcycles and had a fleet of them. He tended to shop for fleets of things. At Graceland, slot-car racing and go-carts were passing obsessions. When he and his group commuted between Memphis and Hollywood, he drove a 1962 Dodge House Car (with kitchen, bedroom, air-conditioning). Later, he commanded a customized Greyhound bus. Eventually Elvis would overcome his fear of flying and buy a fleet of aeroplanes.

Graceland was an elegant, simple limestone house, but Elvis decorated it lavishly, shifting the decor several times over the years. He hated antiques, because they meant dilapidated old furnishings, like those he'd grown up with. He used the knick-knacks and doilies fans sent. He put in deep white carpet and a gold piano in the living room of Graceland, and an *Arabian Nights* decor in the pool room. His bedroom had several TV sets, black-and-white furniture, heavy blue drapes, and a black-velvet ceiling. The TV room in the basement was stark yellow and black, with lightning bolts (inspired by Captain Marvel) painted on the walls. Elvis decorated one room as a practical joke. Vernon had come home one day laughing at some hideous 'jungle' furniture he had seen at a store. Elvis went out and bought it and arranged to have it installed in the den by nightfall – just to see his dad's reaction. A new picture window had to be removed to get some of the heavy, ornate furniture in, and the restaurant tables Vernon had bought from Sears had to go. The new Polynesian-style pieces reminded Elvis of Hawaii, where he had made a movie, and in time, after adding a waterfall and some jungle vines, he grew to like the room, later called the Jungle Room.

There were other suggestions of the jungle at Graceland – a lively, expanding menagerie that included peacocks, burros, monkeys, hogs. Elvis preferred animals that were exotic and amusing. He owned a notoriously lecherous chimp, Scatter, who drank and habitually looked up women's dresses. A mynah bird that 'talked dirty' and said, 'Hey, Gladys!' was exiled after Gladys's death. Late in his life, Elvis invited a pony into the Jungle Room (where it appropriately anointed the rug), just to aggravate his grandmother. As a rule, country people didn't allow animals into the house, but Elvis enjoyed breaking that taboo. He loved dogs, and they had the run of the place. He decorated his house with large dog statues. In later years, Elvis liked to buy all the animals at a pet store and then give them away as presents.

Elvis celebrated his success with excess, lavishing gifts, and people naturally took advantage of his impulsive generosity. Everyone around him was on the Elvis gravy train. The members of the Memphis Mafia were never paid well, but the perks and the glamour of the job made them cancel any other plans whenever Elvis needed his guys. Later on, after they started their families, the guys left their wives and kids behind in Memphis while they went gallivanting with Elvis.

Someone else waited in Memphis. Elvis had brought Priscilla Beaulieu from Germany to live at Graceland and finish high school. Astonishingly, he had sweet-talked her parents into putting their sixteen-year-old daughter in his care. The public didn't know about the relationship. Priscilla was thrilled to move in with her dream man, but before long she began to feel frustrated. Elvis left her at Graceland while he went to Hollywood to make movies and have flings with his leading ladies. His romance with Ann-Margret, his co-star in *Viva Las Vegas*, was his most serious of the decade, and he may have wanted to marry her. But he evidently told her at the outset of their relationship that he had promised to marry Priscilla. Some people thought of Ann-Margret as a twin figure for Elvis because she and Elvis had a similar sensual feeling for music, as well as parallel senses of humour.

Ann-Margret, perceiving Elvis's vulnerability, believed he was just a kid, engulfed by his overwhelming fame.

Priscilla, who was by then eighteen, fumed about the headlines linking Elvis with Ann-Margret. Ann-Margret was vivacious and fun-loving, but also ambitious. Her drive and independence probably challenged Elvis, who believed women should be subordinate. Priscilla, in love with Elvis and lacking experience and a sense of direction, had no goal other than marrying him. She waited for him to make up his mind. But Elvis dawdled.

Although women saw him as strong and macho, with a tender side, and he lived in a tough-guy environment, Elvis was actually a fearful person by nature. He had been afraid of the dark since childhood, and as an adult he felt safer sleeping in the daytime. He lived his life as if he were hiding in a storm shelter, surrounding himself with people who could protect and insulate him. He couldn't bear to be alone. He always had to have someone to sleep with him, and in Hollywood there was no shortage of available women. Early in his career, amazed by his newfound sexual power, he had grabbed at any pretty girl passing by. But in Hollywood, so many women were after him that they had to be screened. Sometimes hives of them swarmed through his house. Apparently Elvis believed sexual prowess was a requisite part of his superstar status, but no one could have sustained that level of performance. In reality, much of the time Elvis just wanted a woman companion nearby; he wanted to know that he wasn't alone.

While waiting for Priscilla to grow up, Elvis worked to mould her into his notion of the ideal woman. Oddly, he tried to make her resemble himself, as though he could fabricate his missing twin. He wanted her hair dyed black, like his; he liked her hair piled high, in an exaggerated female version of his pompadour. It looked more like a haystack. He wanted her to wear heavy eye make-up like Cleopatra's, and he wanted to see her in garish, complicated frocks. Priscilla was compliant; she wanted to be first in his heart, and she would do anything for his approval – just like the guys in Elvis's group.

To casual observers, Elvis must have seemed to be on top of the world. He was rich, handsome, famous. He enjoyed his life. He had friends, he had a place he called home; he rented a luxurious house in Hollywood where he could carry on his fun in his own way. What must Elvis have thought, at waking moments, when he looked around and saw the luxuries he had acquired? At what point did he shift from disbelief to acceptance? Or did he ever? He once said, 'Daddy and I were talking the other night and he said, "El, how did we get here? Last I remember I was working at the paint factory."'

Graceland, with its eighteen rooms, was modest as mansions go, by no means as opulent as movie stars' digs could be. It was a place where the Avon lady came calling, and where an aunt might live in a trailer in the backyard. Although Elvis contributed generously to charities, he hadn't imagined much beyond the lottery winner's dream – cars, mansion, beautiful clothes, more houses. More vehicles. Then what? Elvis had no further vision of what money could do. The basics of food, clothing, transportation, and shelter were the foundation of his material dreams. He spent his money gleefully, aware he was flouting the big dudes. And he gave it away – buying cars and houses and jewellery for people who couldn't afford them, just so he could see the delight on their faces. He knew what it felt like to have nothing and then suddenly hit the jackpot. His generosity began early in his life. Even when he was a small child, he often gave away his toys. When he was five, he gave away his shiny new red wagon. Gladys spanked him and angrily went to retrieve it. She wasn't going to let him throw away her hard-earned money like that.

THE BEATLES

ELVIS WAS LIVING in Hollywood in a Frank Lloyd Wright house rented from the Shah of Iran on 27 August, 1965, the day the Beatles came to visit.

Colonel Parker and Brian Epstein, the Beatles' manager, had been fussing over this arranged meeting for months. The year before, when the Beatles first appeared on T*he Ed Sullivan Show*, the Colonel had sent a telegram from Elvis welcoming them to the United States. The Colonel wanted to remind the world that Elvis – *his* boy, the biggest moneymaker in Hollywood – was the reigning King of Rock-and-Roll. But that seemed in doubt. Beatlemania ruled the airwaves by then. Two weeks earlier, the Beatles had played to sixty-five thousand fans at Shea Stadium – a record-breaking number. Only a few years after Elvis emerged, rock-and-roll fever had spread, and now the Beatles were at the forefront of what would soon become known as the cultural revolution of the sixties. While Elvis was making vacuous formula movies, an explosion of rock-and-roll energy was supplying the soundtrack to another major cultural shift.

Apprehensive about the challenge the Beatles posed, Elvis tried to avoid the meeting, but finally he capitulated. He felt threatened by the Beatles. They were exciting and quick-witted, with musical talent that was fresh and charged. Yet he was their idol. They were fans come to pay homage. 'We all wanted to be Elvis,' John Lennon said of the group's beginnings. 'Before Elvis, there was nothing.'

Elvis had a new single out, 'I'm Yours' and '(It's a) Long Lonely Highway', both songs recorded years before. His current album was called *Elvis for Everyone*, with a cover picture of a cash register and the RCA trademark dog, Nipper. The Beatles' new album, *Help!*, an energetic sound-track to their new movie, was innovative and adventurous, and they had even written their own songs. The Beatles had, apparently with little effort, tossed off two original, charming movies that won critical acclaim and box-office success – *A Hard Day's Night* and then *Help!*. Elvis's current movie was *Tickle Me*, a lame frolic set at a beauty spa, and he had just finished filming arguably his worst movie, *Frankie and Johnny*, a period riverboat-gambling melodrama. He was discouraged about his film career, sick of paper-thin plots and mindless soundtrack songs. He was just about to begin filming *Paradise, Hawaiian Style*.

The meeting of Elvis and the Beatles has been documented from several viewpoints, and some of the recollections are at variance. Elvis was surrounded by his gang of guys, some with their wives and girlfriends – all of whom had to subdue their bubbling excitement so as not to offend Elvis. Priscilla, then twenty years old, was present. The meeting was elaborately and secretly arranged, yet fans mobbed the gates when the Beatles arrived at the modern Oriental-style house on Perugia Way in Bel Air.

The Beatles couldn't speak at first; they were in awe. The scene was awkward, so Elvis picked up the TV remote control and started changing channels. The Beatles were impressed by the gadget, the first such they had seen. Elvis, on a long, white L-shaped couch, said, 'If you guys are just gonna sit there and stare at me, I'm going to bed. I didn't mean for this to be like the subjects calling on the King. I just thought we'd sit and talk about music and maybe jam a little.'

A jukebox was playing, and Elvis picked up a bass guitar and strummed along with Charlie Rich's 'Mohair Sam'. Some more guitars appeared, and John Lennon and Paul McCartney played with Elvis – a historic jam session, but short-lived, only a song or two. Some present hardly remembered it afterwards, while some believed it had lasted much longer.

Elvis bristled when Lennon asked why he did not make any more rock-and-roll records. 'I loved the Sun records,' Lennon said. Elvis became defensive. The evening, already strained, grew tenser, and it drifted. George Harrison was quiet, and he ended up by the pool smoking a joint with one of Elvis's guys. Ringo Starr seemed to enjoy himself, playing roulette with the Colonel.

The next day, John Lennon told Jerry Schilling, one of the Memphis Mafia, that the evening had meant a lot to him and asked him to tell Elvis that 'if it hadn't been for him we would have been nothing'. Lennon said to Marty Lacker, another of the guys, 'Last night was the greatest night of my life.' Possibly Lennon passed these belated compliments to assuage his own embarrassment, or to apologize. His manner was aggressive and cheeky, the opposite of Elvis's. During the evening, kidding around, he had played the role of Inspector Clouseau, and two or three times he had challenged Elvis, apparently rather rudely. Lennon rubbed Elvis the wrong way, and some have suggested that this was partly behind Elvis's later denunciation of the Beatles as unwholesome for the youth of America.

Approval from the Beatles, the upstarts challenging his position, made him uncomfortable. He was their hero, which placed a great burden on him to live up to their image of him. And accepting their admiration meant accepting them as his judges, authorities whose judgement might easily turn against him. John Lennon was called the 'intellectual Beatle' – he had even written a couple of widely admired books. He was a figure sure to intimidate an insecure Southerner, no matter how many records he had sold.

They departed from the Perugia Way house with boxes of Elvis records, gifts bestowed by the Colonel. Earlier he had sent them cowboy outfits and six-shooters and little covered wagons that lit up. A covered wagon was his logo, evoking his carnival days. And what did the Beatles make of all that? When they got back to England, what did they do with their covered-wagon lamps and their six-shooters? The illuminated covered wagon on Elvis's mantel in his Bel Air house had a sign printed on it: ALL THE WAY WITH LBJ.

The Beatles were disappointed in their idol. If Elvis had been truly secure in his role, he could have welcomed them more graciously and generously. He could have taken pride in the contribution he had made to the Beatles' own art and to the growth of a powerful music. He could have taken credit for setting in motion something that was bigger than himself. Then they could have banged those guitars together till broad daylight. But Elvis wasn't ready to act the elder statesman.

Time was passing Elvis by, and he knew it. He liked some of the early Beatles music and identified with it, but later on, when they began to experiment, they lost him. They must have seemed arrogant and in the know about things he couldn't share. The entire counterculture movement of the sixties, which they came to exemplify within a few years, was beyond Elvis. He couldn't identify with the angst of middle-class kids jolted by the Vietnam War. He had been in the Army and done his duty, and he couldn't join the youth rebellion against the establishment. As an outsider, he had tried too hard to get in. He couldn't turn down the amenities he had once been deprived of; he affirmed the society the counterculture rebelled against.

The evening in 1965 would have been confusing and upsetting to Elvis, who had once been criticized as a dangerous rebel rocker. He had been the trailblazer – without any role model to guide him. Rock-and-roll had flowed out of his youthful soul spontaneously. He virtually invented the sound and stance and demeanour of the rock-and-roll star. But now he wanted to blaze more trails, venture into new musical directions. Rock-and-roll was never the only music he loved; it reflected only one portion of his soul. When the Beatles came to visit him, he must have cringed inside in humiliation, thinking of how he had compromised his career by languishing in Hollywood. The Beatles had redefined the film musical, with songs that were natural to the plot and not arbitrary, artificial outbursts, as they were in Elvis's movies. Elvis knew he could do better – if he had the chance.

HOLLYWEIRD

IN APRIL 1964, Elvis was devastated to read in a trade-news column that producer Hal Wallis was using his lucrative Presley movies to finance less commercial, more artistic works like *Becket*, a drama about the friendship between the Archbishop of Canterbury and Henry II. The movie starred Richard Burton and Peter O'Toole. Elvis had aspired to be in that league, and now this comment by Hal Wallis made him feel a fool, as if everyone knew a secret that he didn't. Elvis felt he was being used.

Elvis loved movies. Singing came easily to him; it was always a natural part of his life, whatever his circumstances. While growing up, he had dreamed of being a singing star, but the movies had always occupied another realm of his ambition – an almost hallucinatory escape from the dreariness of poverty. Now that he had the chance to be in the movies, he wanted to be a serious actor, like Burton or O'Toole, but after starring in a number of movies, he was deeply disappointed in himself that he had not made a critically acclaimed film. He had not even been allowed the opportunity. And as the sixties continued, his material did not improve. The Colonel snubbed any offer of a quality picture. Acting on Elvis's behalf, the Colonel turned down *Thunder Road*, *West Side Story*, and *Midnight Cowboy*, to name a few. He believed Elvis's success in movies depended on his singing. He had a clear notion that the greatest box-office appeal would be to the lowest common denominator. The Colonel knew the carnival crowd inside and out, and Elvis was his trick pony.

Elvis sang comfortable songs in placid stories about a singer's rise to fame or banal tales about some upstanding hunk plagued by problems as trivial as static on the radio. The settings changed, but Elvis's magic endured, movie to movie. His movies, star vehicles, depended purely on his charisma. Since millions of fans loved Elvis unquestioningly, the Colonel saw no need for good music, good plots, or good acting. For several years, the fans who bought most of the tickets to these movies imbibed their idol without complaint. Whatever he did in the plot, whatever silly costume he wore, however false his lines, the fans didn't care. He was Elvis and they just wanted to feast their eyes and ears.

It's easy to dismiss Elvis's movies – vacuous, bland puddings filled with jingles and ditties. Although a few – such as *Jailhouse Rock*, *King Creole*, and *Wild in the Country* – attempt moral complexity, most of them are predictable portrayals of Elvis as a contemporary Adonis with girl trouble. They are awful, yet seductive. His uncritical fans were on to something. When you glimpse one of these movies now on a late-night TV channel, you're brought up short at the sight of Elvis, with his slim figure in his well-fitting jeans (he thought of jeans as a costume, not a garment of choice). He may be stilted and unnatural – waterskiing or strumming a guitar surrounded by a gaggle of girls at a swimming pool – but his smouldering sexuality comes through. You can look past the scripted moves, the phoney set-ups, the unnatural beauties. Moving through the cheap showbiz props, Elvis is spellbinding: his sensuous mouth, his good humour, his perfect profile, his Mississippi drawl (straightened out somewhat). You always sense the artificiality of his jet-black hair, but it doesn't seem to matter. He looks good.

Elvis had started his film career hopefully, with some serious roles. *Jailhouse Rock* (1957) trumpeted Elvis's rebel image. In *King Creole* (1958), recognized as Elvis's best dramatic role, he plays another misfit version of himself. But later, the challenge to propriety and values that he had represented in the fifties was no longer the focus, and serious themes are scarce. In *Viva Las Vegas* (1964) he's a race-car driver. In *Tickle Me* (1965) he's a rodeo rider at a resort who keeps breaking into song, thrilling all the girls at their calisthenics.

Frankie and Johnny (1966), a prime example of how the quality of his movies deteriorated, is empty and ludicrous – to put it mildly. Elvis looks great, still young and trim, and he wears some handsome marching-band outfits. But he performs some of the up-tempo songs with such minimal moves that he seems in danger of losing his Elvis licence. The ante-bellum story involves entertainers on a gambling river-boat. Three women dressed as Madame Pompadour go to a costume ball. In his riverboat-gambler suit, Johnny, our hero, serenades Frankie with a romantic ballad. The movie ends happily when the fated bullet dents a cricket pendant on Johnny's chest instead of his heart.

Flaming Star, in 1960, after the Army, was a film Elvis had hopes for, especially because it had been written for Marlon Brando. Elvis played a half-breed Indian torn between cultures. On the set of *Flaming Star*, filmed on a desert ranch in California, Elvis warmed up each morning with karate exercises. He had become a karate enthusiast in Germany. A friend of mine was an extra in that movie, and he told me, 'Elvis had sparring matches with his Memphis buddies and knocked them around pretty soundly. He drew a big audience (among the movie folk) for these warm-ups. Part of the exercises consisted of breaking two-by-fours. I remember telling him that he should market two-by-fours as Elvis karate boards, and he said Colonel Parker had already thought of that. He went ahead and used some karate in the movie, about as out of place and out of date as you can get.'

From the start, Elvis was a charming presence on a Hollywood set. He worked hard and was always on time, and one veteran after another claimed Elvis was the nicest person they had ever worked with. For his first movie, *Love Me Tender*, in 1956, he impressed everyone on the set by showing up with the script memorized – everyone's lines, including his own. Often the people on the sets of his movies found him so mesmerizing that no one, not even the director, would approach him with any tips to help him be a better actor. He got away with bad acting because people around him actually couldn't tell, they were so snowed by him. Elvis had found no need for singing lessons, and he felt acting lessons might stifle his natural talent. The Colonel, satisfied with the sure-fire formulaic movies, saw no need for Elvis to learn the craft of acting. 'They'll never win any Academy Awards,' the Colonel said. 'All they're good for is to make money.' He kept production costs down, sometimes limiting the shooting time to two or three weeks.

Elvis's music suffered. For a couple of years after the Army, he recorded some hit songs (such as 'Are You Lonesome Tonight?', 'Good Luck Charm', and 'Return to Sender') in the style he had made famous, and some gospel music that he poured his soul into, but the Colonel, as usual, rationed Elvis's exposure, steering him towards the movie soundtrack albums, because the big money was in the movies. Moreover, the Colonel used the mostly lacklustre soundtrack albums to fulfil Elvis's recording contract with RCA, thus minimizing the studio work in which Elvis would have developed his musical ideas. For several years in the sixties he was limited to only a few studio albums. While the rock-and-roll revolution he had initiated rolled on, Elvis was stuck in a rut.

Long after he realized that he was being used, he behaved as if he had to do the movies and soundtracks. Theoretically Elvis handled the artistic end of the job and the Colonel made the deals. While the Colonel may have suffered from blind ignorance of artistic sensibility, he was devoted to his job as he saw it. Elvis was his only client, his *raison d'être*, his identity. From the beginning, whenever Elvis fretted over being told what to do, the Colonel pointedly reminded him how easily he could be dashed back into poverty: it could all be taken away overnight and he would be driving a truck in Memphis again.

In later years, Elvis was angry, seething at the Colonel much of the time. But whenever he tried to get out of a contract, the Colonel would say something irrefutable and Elvis would give in. Some observers suggest that the Colonel had a few things to blackmail Elvis with – his live-in child girlfriend, for example, and later, his abuse of prescription pills. Whether or not the Colonel held a club over his head, he was able to portray Elvis's finances in such a way as to show him that he couldn't afford to quit making movies. Elvis's father always persuaded him to stick with the Colonel.

Elvis was caught in a trap. Even though he wanted to be a serious actor, he was afraid to risk bucking the money-making formula. He frequently sabotaged his own efforts at independence by splurging. By spending, he kept his illusion of control and endless wealth. But he came close to bankruptcy several times, further obligating him to continue making the movies. Since the Colonel made three-picture deals, Elvis's future was always in hock.

Why did Elvis let the Colonel have such power over him? Simply, the Colonel was his boss. In the context of Elvis's world, when you come from poverty, you cannot turn down a hundred and fifty thousand dollars, no matter what you have to do for it. And this is a key to Elvis's attitude. His predicament was an inevitable result of his aspirations. He was innocently authentic, but he craved the inauthentic, as country people, who are so close – uncomfortably close – to what is starkly real, often do. For him, the bright artificial lights of the city, flashy cars, and fat rolls of cash represented the values of the dominant social classes. They were the emblems of success. He wasn't a firebrand. He didn't seize the opportunity for protest (as Bob Dylan, for instance, did, by focusing on dust-bowl classics). Elvis behaved like many other poor Southerners, accepting the heel of oppression when they should have been thinking more radically. This is characteristic Southern passivity and fatalism, which often belies an inner fire – a rebel sneer, at least.

And Elvis had plenty of inner fire. It had come out in his music and in his personal behaviour. Back in 1956, the humiliation Elvis had suffered in New York activated his pride, his desire to be his true self in the face of authority. But now his passion was sublimated as he conceded power to the man to whom he owed his success. His overt passivity was partly his own nature and partly his Mississippi background. He had learned subservience from his parents and from the culture. And his religion taught humility before a higher master. So Elvis served God, parents, and the bigwigs in Hollywood, even though he thought Hollywood was full of phoneys. He called it 'Hollyweird'. But he battled internally and let out his frustrations in diverse ways. In his private life, he manipulated people and usually managed to get his own way. His renowned temper expressed his frustration when he was unable to be manfully in control. Lamar Fike, one of the Memphis Mafia, said, 'Elvis would carry an anvil for thirty years for you if you asked him nicely, but if you told him to do it he'd tell you where to stick it.' This kind of rebellion, the immature childish fits of temper that Elvis was subject to, was not a true use of his power – not the kind of power a secure person would exert.

The roots of Elvis's behaviour run even deeper into Southern culture. His parents were children of sharecroppers.

Vernon himself had worked as a sharecropper in the early years of his marriage. A plantation sharecropper growing cotton on a fifty-fifty share would pay half the expenses, and when the boss man paid the tenant for the crop, he would deduct the advance – which might be an arbitrary amount for food and clothing provided to the tenant. The bottom line might be less than a third of the sharecropper's half of the crop. The tenant might have the illusion of sharing the profits, but in reality the boss man made the rules.

Elvis got himself in such a situation of debt servitude with Colonel Parker. Elvis was sharecropping his own talent. By the time the Colonel deducted his expenses and raked in the money from his side deals, Elvis may have made even less than the Colonel. But the important fact was that Elvis couldn't leave. The boss man kept him dependent. Elvis's behaviour – regardless of the details – was like that of the sharecropper. He just had a different boss man from the one he might have had if he had stayed in the Mississippi of his youth.

In 1967, at the nadir of his Hollywood career, Elvis recorded bluesman Jimmy Reed's 'Big Boss Man', a song that helped to revive his rock-and-roll spirit. It was a true story of his life. Elvis's great power as a cultural force is that in an original fashion, he transcended the boss men of the world. But it was a state of mind that he could not sustain in his own personal life.

In Hollywood, Elvis was on a gerbil play-wheel. His profligacy was like that of people in Mississippi at the juke joints on a Saturday night, blowing the week's pay. The lifestyle was self-perpetuating as long as he stayed on the wheel in his cage. But Elvis, still a dreamer, always hoped for the possibility of better material. Serious directors like Nicholas Ray and George Cukor wanted Elvis, but the Colonel stood guard. Early on, the Colonel's pet project for Elvis was a movie about the life of the country singer Hank Williams. He got a director interested, but the deal eventually fell through. It's unlikely that Elvis was eager to make a film about a star who was an alcoholic and who only a few years before had been subjected to many of the same pressures of fame that Elvis was. Williams's story was depressing and ended badly when, in 1953, at the age of twenty-nine, he died of an overdose of prescription pills.

But as the decade wore on, Elvis more and more placed his own faith in prescription pills. He had started with amphetamines, and they were always handy for the long drives between Memphis and Los Angeles and for the early studio calls. But as time went by, he needed tranquillizers to bring him down far enough to get to sleep, and then more uppers to recharge his batteries the next day.

This way, Elvis kept going, but he didn't know where.

QUEST

ELVIS WAS READING. In the middle of 1964, it became a chronic complaint of those around him. All of a sudden, Elvis wasn't interested in anything fun. Instead of renting the movie theatre for the night, or frolicking at the fairgrounds, he was likely to be sitting in bed with his books. Instead of having parties and jam sessions, Elvis was studying. Even when they travelled, he lugged along trunkloads of books. A wave of impatience and concern rolled through the Elvis camp.

Elvis had always liked books. For his fourteenth birthday, his father gave him a book by *New Yorker* cartoonist George Price – a surprisingly sophisticated selection for Vernon to have made. Elvis's favourite subject in school was English, and he worked in the library. He always felt a need to educate himself further, to improve himself. A 1963 receipt for books sent to Graceland from a shop in Memphis included titles that ranged from *Giants of Science* and *East of Eden* to *World Philosophy* and *Vocabulary Builder*. For about a month, Elvis even conducted a vocabulary class for his entourage.

In 1964, he began a serious study of the world's faiths. Among other things, he was studying Eastern philosophy. He was practising meditation long before the Beatles went to India to see the Maharishi Mahesh Yogi.

As his movie projects got sillier, Elvis felt an excruciating dissatisfaction with himself, and he struggled to understand the meaning of his extraordinary success. The knot of deep pain inside of him – stemming from the loss of his twin and from his own sensitive nature – never left him. He still blushed and stuttered and felt like an outsider. The death of his mother, who had given him the only sense of security he had ever had, compounded his pain. He felt something of a fraud. Why had he been chosen to receive such acclaim and riches? To become an idol? For Elvis, the burning question was 'Why am I Elvis? Why was I picked to be Elvis Presley?' He couldn't imagine that his tremendous popularity might have been simply the result of talent and ambition and hard work and random circumstances. How could he account for the adoration, the heavy rucksacks of fan mail, the sensational hit records? He could still make fun of his image, but he felt responsible to it – privileged by it and also burdened by it. He believed he had been chosen for a mission. But what mission? What should he do? What did it mean to be treated so worshipfully? Did he deserve it?

From the beginning of his fame and on through the sixties, while he toiled in the industry of illusion, these questions plagued him. In his quest for spiritual enlightenment, Elvis dabbled in every kind of faith and belief, reading hungrily through all the world's religions and finding something either comfortingly familiar or satisfyingly esoteric in each. He had long wrestled with the religion of his youth – the Holiness sect of Pentecostalism, the Assembly of God. The fire-and-brimstone sermons had terrified him in childhood, and now the minister in Memphis was always wanting money from him. All his life, Elvis had been deeply spiritual, but he had backed away from the literalness and absolutism of his church's beliefs – such as that movies were sinful. When his father took him to his first movie, they had to make sure the church didn't find out. Still, Elvis's native superstitiousness – typical among country people – made him susceptible to off-the-wall ideas. If a black cat crossed his path, he'd turn back to avoid bad luck. His mother had believed in the supernatural, and Elvis always thought she had mystical powers.

Elvis was encouraged in his spiritual journey by a chance encounter – on 30 April, 1964 – with an unlikely source, a young hairdresser named Larry Geller, who had a spiritual bent and eclectic interests – yoga, metaphysics, meditation, numerology, cryptograms, the *I Ching*, Islamic art, the Rosicrucians. He gave Elvis some books: *The Impersonal Life*, *Autobiography of a Yogi*, *The Initiation of the World*, and *Beyond the Himalayas*. Characteristically, Elvis jumped in with both feet. Geller spoke seriously about the purpose of life and self-discovery, and Elvis evidently found him to be the first person he had met since his mother's death with whom he could speak about the turmoil in his soul. This was Elvis's first real break through the bubble in which he had been living. Geller wrote in his book, '*If I Can Dream*': *Elvis' Own Story*, 'What touched off Elvis's spiritual crisis and made his search so all-consuming was his life. It was apparent that he felt stranded by both his disenchantment with his religious education and the vacuousness of the lifestyle that fame had thrust upon him.'

Elvis was overjoyed to discover a person who could talk thoughtfully about a wide range of ideas. Geller, whom Elvis began to call his 'guru', had a different sort of mind from any of the others in the group. The men Elvis had around him were facilitators, buddies, not thinkers or soul-searchers. From their point of view, Geller's intrusion into the group was sinister. They pegged him for a fraud and a loony and suspected him of practising New Age voodoo on Elvis's mind. They were even afraid Geller was trying to get Elvis to be a cult leader. Geller became a regular in Elvis's group, even though he was treated with hostility. The others saw something frenetic and lunatic in Elvis's new enthusiasms, and they felt that his strange pursuits distracted him from the jazzy life they were accustomed to, as well as from his work. Priscilla, who was frantic to marry Elvis, was bored out of her skull with his new passions. And she seemed afraid of where his new interests might take him. She complained that with his spiritual studies, Elvis had lost his vibrant personality and reverted to passivity. She and Elvis had many arguments about his books, but he was serious about them.

Elvis rapidly began to expand his interests, trying to find some order and sense in the jumble of his mind. He began an all-out earnest pursuit of the answers, willing to try any new idea. He became a member of Paramahansa Yogananda's Self-Realization Fellowship (the woman who was his guru resembled his mother). Inspired by the idyllic setting of the

Self-Realization Fellowship Park in Pacific Palisades, he created a Meditation Garden at Graceland. He turned his nightly gatherings into philosophy classrooms; he made everybody read Timothy Leary's *Psychedelic Experience*; he annotated mystical books with personal observations. With Geller, Elvis hunted for forbidden messages hidden in Shakespeare with the same scholarly fervour that Beatles fans studied 'I Am the Walrus'. He was desperate to have a vision. And, as always, he wanted a quick fix.

Eventually, in March 1965, he did have a vision – the figure of Joseph Stalin emerged from a cloud outside Flagstaff, Arizona. 'Why Stalin? Of all people, what's he doing up there?' Elvis asked Larry Geller, who was travelling with him. Elvis saw the Stalin image as the dark side of himself, and as he watched, Stalin turned into Jesus and Elvis felt himself in the presence of God.

With that, Elvis decided to become a monk. But it was a wistful notion. The filming of *Harum Scarum*, a frivolous romp with Rudolph Valentino-like costumes, began soon, and Elvis found himself back at work, convinced he should share his special gifts with the world instead of retreating to a monastery. Elvis realized he couldn't give up being Elvis. For all the pain it caused him, he loved being Elvis. His real quest was to find some way of rationalizing and living with the embarrassments and inadequacies of his life; he needed some justification and reassurance that he was all right.

After his vision, Elvis's insular existence took a quirky turn. He saw angels and UFOs in the bushes. Sometimes, stoned on pills, he stood on the coffee table and preached lengthy, hilarious sermons to the guys – who were not encouraged to laugh. According to Billy Smith, 'He'd say something like "Moses was this white-haired son of a bitch who came down from the mountain. The burning bushes directed his ass on down." '

Everyone found Elvis's behaviour bizarre. His visions and preachings were no doubt enhanced by the uppers and downers he was taking. Even so, the people around him must have failed to comprehend a crucial thing about him – the extent of his own private struggle with the image of Elvis. Elvis had been visited by an incomprehensible experience – his fame – and he was blinded by it. His earnest quest became the essence of his story. He suffered extensive guilt because of his failure to live up to the ideal. He was profligate, manipulative, self-indulgent. He even cheated on his self-realization programme. Too impatient to go through the prescribed disciplines, he connived to be given its secrets before he had earned the right.

The popular hero in our age struggles with fame. Caught in the arms of his lover – Celebrity – he cannot withdraw prematurely. He wants to go all the way, and yet he knows he should retreat and become a monk. He strives for a balancing act: the desire for recognition and the desire for anonymity. From time to time, Elvis flirted half-heartedly with the idea of giving up his career. When someone reminded him that he wouldn't be Elvis any more, he dropped the idea. But late in life he even hatched a short-lived plan to switch identities with a terminally ill man.

'I get so tired of being Elvis Presley,' he said more than once.

Elvis carried his religious impulses into the recording

studio. By the end of 1965, his movies were waning in popularity, and the Colonel and RCA decided it was time Elvis recorded a studio album. In mid-1965, his single 'Crying in the Chapel' (actually recorded in 1960) went to number three on the charts; it was the first big hit he had had in a couple of years, and its spiritual nature renewed his interest in making music that aimed higher than the soundtrack albums he had been churning out.

He recorded in Nashville, in May 1966, with a new producer, Felton Jarvis, who brought fresh energy to the sessions. Elvis plunged into recording some spiritual and gospel songs – classics like 'In the Garden', 'Farther Along', and 'Where Could I Go But to the Lord'. But the centrepiece was 'How Great Thou Art', which Elvis sang beautifully, with all the feeling generated by his spiritual journey and with the expertise saved up from years of singing spiritual music at home.

The session didn't produce any pop hit material, but the album *How Great Thou Art*, released in 1967, earned Elvis his first Grammy award – for Best Sacred Performance.

THE FLYING CIRCLE G

ELVIS LOVED PLANS and projects, and he threw himself intensely into anything new. In 1967, he launched into a venture that might have offered a calm and healthful resolution of his anxious spiritual quest. He went back to nature.

On a country drive outside of Memphis, Elvis and Priscilla had spotted a lighted sixty-five-foot cross on a lovely, rolling piece of land. It appeared to Elvis as a signal to his destiny. The farm was for sale, and impulsively he bought it – at an inflated price that almost gave Vernon a heart attack ('Oh, Lordy!').

By then Elvis and Priscilla were engaged. After postponing for as long as possible, Elvis had finally given in, and he proposed to Priscilla just before Christmas. They had been riding horses frequently, so it seemed sensible to have a retreat from busy Graceland. The 160-acre ranch was in Walls, Mississippi, near Memphis. 'Good God, I've moved back to Mississippi!' Elvis said in chagrin.

Elvis named the ranch the Flying Circle G (after

Graceland) and began a spending spree that almost bankrupted him. He had a dream of a commune, with all his guys settled in together – this time with wives and children, who usually were not part of his Hollywood encampment. He bought everybody a house trailer and arranged the trailers in a circle around the small lake. He bought everybody a horse and a truck. He bought thirteen pick-up trucks in one day. He got himself a tractor. He put in fencing and a pre-fab security house. He built a bridge over a pond. He bought a black Welsh pony. He went to Sears' basement himself and stocked up on power tools. The only house on the property was an old brick cottage, situated on a highway intersection; in no time the narrow lawn was knee-deep in fans and curiosity seekers. Although Priscilla was delighted with the cottage and called it her dream home, Elvis decided he'd rather live in a double-wide trailer, with a white picket fence. He and Priscilla played house in the double-wide, and she cooked for him. The secret to cooking for Elvis, she learned, was to burn everything.

For the whole gang, it was an idyllic period while it lasted. They had fun, and some of the guys began to feel they were at last settling down comfortably with their families. They had good times – horseback riding, picnics, and group singing every night.

While Elvis may have entertained fantasies of getting in touch with the earth and the seasons, it turned out that he couldn't really relate to nature except artificially. At the ranch, he managed to be up and about during daylight hours, but the thrill of spending money on the ranch seemed greater than the quiet pleasures and commitments of ranching.

Wearing a cowboy outfit, he rode horseback with a bag of hot-dog buns hooked on the saddle horn. He munched them continually. He was gaining weight and behaving even more impetuously than usual. He seemed addled and confused by the uppers and downers he was taking in greater quantities.

Elvis was trying to exert his own power in the only way he knew how, by taking control of his immediate daily life – acting out his instincts for generosity and grand schemes. He rebelled against his movie obligations by indulging in riotous spending sprees, but ironically the spending shut him more tightly in his prison. At the ranch, Elvis was avoiding having to go back to Hollywood and make yet another trifling movie, *Clambake*.

The Colonel had perceived Elvis to be drifting away from his true mission of cranking out profitable movies, and the movies themselves were starting to decline in popularity. Although Elvis's spiritual album, *How Great Thou Art*, sold steadily, the latest movie soundtrack, *Easy Come, Easy Go*, was hardly worth humming. Priscilla said Elvis was 'despondent over *Clambake*' and so gained weight.

Elvis didn't appear in California on time to begin *Clambake* and instead had to dash to Nashville to record the soundtrack. He recorded half-heartedly – empty tunes like 'Who Needs Money?' and 'Confidence' – then rushed back to the ranch, where a quarter mile of temporary plywood fencing was being installed for privacy. But before long, he reluctantly trekked to California.

Soon after Elvis arrived to begin production of *Clambake*, he fell in his bathroom and suffered a minor concussion.

Probably drugs had made him clumsy. The Colonel, taking advantage of Elvis's condition, stepped in to restore some order and focus to his client by firing some of Elvis's guys. He also tried to put a stop to 'his involvement with esoteric philosophies'. Priscilla wrote in her memoir that the Colonel 'put a halt to the soul-searching' because it was interfering with Elvis's career.

The Colonel said, 'I don't want him reading any more books! They clutter up his mind.' He said to the guys, 'Some of you think maybe he's Jesus Christ who should wear robes and walk down the street helping people. But that's not who he is.'

And he forbade Larry Geller to spend any time alone with Elvis. After that, the remaining guys – who had always been suspicious – became openly hostile to Geller, and Geller bowed out eventually. Elvis had always defended him when the guys teased him – they called him 'Swami' and made fun of his vegetarianism – but when the Colonel denounced him, Elvis didn't stand up for him. Even though their new contract gave the Colonel even more power, with grand opportunities for profit-sharing, Elvis still trusted him. He appreciated the way the Colonel could snow the Hollywood phoneys without compromising himself. Elvis seemed to take pleasure in the Colonel's exploits and still felt beholden to him, even as he railed against the insipid movie scripts.

On 1 May, 1967, three days after he finished filming *Clambake*, Elvis and Priscilla were married in Las Vegas. The wedding was hastily and secretly arranged by the Colonel, who had been pressuring them to go ahead with their plans. Elvis and Priscilla were whisked abruptly through the ceremony and reception and hardly seemed to understand what was happening. And there were hard feelings among the crew about who got invited and what roles were played. There was no real honeymoon. Back at Graceland a month later, Elvis and Priscilla donned their wedding duds again and hosted a reception for their friends.

There are varying reports about why Elvis didn't marry Priscilla sooner and what role the Colonel played. The Colonel probably urged the hasty marriage to avoid a scandal erupting over Elvis's live-in girlfriend. Some say Elvis did not want to get married at all. He had developed a bachelor-commune lifestyle that did not always include her. He hadn't been able to commit himself to the idea of being a husband and father, even though he wanted to in the abstract. Yet Elvis was also a good boy, and he must have remembered how his mother wanted him to marry and give her grandchildren. However he went astray, Elvis struggled to do what was right. He felt responsible for Priscilla, having settled her at Graceland and cared for her until she became an adult. And apparently, years before, when he brought her to Memphis, he had promised her parents he would marry her.

According to Priscilla, they had not gone 'all the way' until their wedding night. And then she immediately became pregnant. Priscilla and Elvis always had fun together, we are told, and he loved to try to make her laugh. They behaved like lovebirds, and Priscilla said she always felt Elvis was her strong protector. Although most people who were around them insist that Elvis really loved Priscilla, there is something deeply dispiriting about this marriage. He was in charge of her, becoming her surrogate father when she was still a teenager. He believed women should be dominated and should not pursue careers. Yet the women who had fired him up the most had challenged him with their spunk and independence. Priscilla grew to be outspoken, too, but at the beginning she was too young to have developed much individuality. And she perhaps turned out to be less a romance than a kid sister – as Elvis later remarked.

That summer, committed to yet another jejune movie, *Speedway*, Elvis lost interest in the Flying Circle G ranch, and by the end of the year he had auctioned off his purchases. (Eventually he sold the ranch.) He and Priscilla bought a secluded home in Los Angeles, and Priscilla – pregnant – busied herself with decorating what she hoped would be a real home, without a dozen guys living with them.

Shortly after their wedding, Priscilla had persuaded Elvis to burn his books, and they had a bonfire at Graceland of many of them. Elvis, now that they were married, tried to appease Priscilla, but he was unable to stop his spiritual search. Five years later, in 1972, when Larry Geller was reinstated in the group, he was pleased to see that Elvis was still involved in what he called the 'teachings' and was surrounded by mystical books. Elvis especially liked a biography of spiritualist Madame Blavatsky, because she looked like Gladys. Elvis told Geller that on the day in the desert when he had his Stalin-Jesus vision, its significance seemed to explode inside him. Elvis saw himself as Jesus; inside he was Elvis Christ. He didn't believe he was the reincarnation of Jesus, but a version of him, another Christ with a special purpose on earth. Geller reported in his book,

'*If I Can Dream*', that Elvis told him he felt crucified with his knowledge, carrying it around secretly for years. It was the holiest moment of his life, he said, but he felt that Priscilla would have him locked up if she only knew what he was grappling with. 'I was hanging on my own cross,' Elvis said. 'It took a long time to figure it all out, how Elvis fit into the big picture.' But eventually, he claimed, everything fell into place for him. He understood then that he was an entertainer and his mission was to help people – not as a preacher, because that wasn't his talent, but as a singer. His mission was to get across the message of love through his songs.

'THE COMEBACK SPECIAL'

EVEN THE COLONEL knew it was time for a change. With movie profits plummeting and Elvis's interest in making the movies ever dwindling, something had to happen. *Speedway* barely recovered production costs. Record sales were also still in decline.

Many of the fans were begging him to give up the movies and tour again. Elvis needed some fresh music. The same thing had happened with his recordings as with the movies – he got lousy material. The singer-songwriter trend dominated now, and artists such as John Lennon and Paul McCartney wanted to keep the full rights to their own songs when other musicians recorded them. But the Colonel had always demanded a share of the songwriter's royalties as well as a share in the publishing rights to songs Elvis recorded. His deal with Hill and Range Publishers limited Elvis's choices of songs to the material it gathered. So Elvis had little chance of recording anything from outside that stable.

Elvis, with no impulse to write his own music, loved singing and interpreting songs his own way. He loved the thrill of harmonizing with other voices, especially on gospel songs. But his efforts often seemed to be sabotaged. Again and again, after he had worked on a song to perfection, record company technicians mixed the song differently, so that what he heard on the release was different from what he had endorsed in the studio. This loss of artistic control angered him. He knew the Colonel was meddling, and he felt helpless.

But when he recorded 'Big Boss Man' and 'Guitar Man', an upbeat Jerry Reed song, in late 1967, his spirits rose. Although the single of 'Big Boss Man' reached only number thirty-eight on the charts, the recording session, in Nashville, had stirred Elvis as nothing in the studio had in a long while. After a long period of lethargy and dissatisfaction with cranking out soundtrack albums, Elvis seemed to find the spark he needed to pull out of his funk. He realized it was now or never – get moving again or sink into oblivion. The Nashville session reignited his hopes of making good music.

Before long, Elvis was able to leave Hollywood, to walk away from the brain-rotting movies. The opportunity arose in 1968, when NBC proposed a TV special. For the first time in seven years, Elvis was going to perform onstage before an audience. The young producer, Steve Binder, was intent on resurrecting the lost Elvis, and he had a specific vision for the show: a stripping away of the movie-star Elvis and a return to the Elvis who had revolutionized popular music – the original rebel rocker, with the dark, threatening image. Although the Colonel envisioned the show as a tame Christmas special with songs like 'The Little Drummer Boy' and 'Santa Claus Is Coming to Town', Binder had no intention of letting this unique chance for Elvis to do his real stuff be smothered by a sentimental formula.

As Elvis immersed himself in the project, the Colonel stewed on the sidelines, but he didn't interfere this time. He knew they had to go in a new direction; the movie formula no longer worked. As he did in 1956, the Colonel turned to TV for exposure. For Elvis, the TV special was a daring move, occurring so soon after the Beatles' *Sgt Pepper's Lonely Hearts Club Band* had redefined popular music by blurring the boundary between low art and high art. The Beatles, almost playfully, had challenged popular art to grow and had challenged highbrow audiences to pay attention to lowbrow possibility. Elvis made his bravest decision of the decade. He jumped up and reclaimed his title.

The show followed a storyline, the journey of the 'Guitar Man' through success, corruption, and salvation. The thematic structure was based on a classic story, *The Blue Bird*, by the Belgian playwright Maurice Maeterlinck. The show consisted of several production numbers alternating with songs from an informal jam session that had been filmed separately before a studio audience. The jam session was the best part of the show. For that, Elvis had recruited his original musicians, Scotty Moore and drummer D. J. Fontana. (Bill Black had died.) Elvis's form-fitting black leather suit was an unforgettable costume, the essence of Elvis the rocker. With his wicked black hair, Elvis appeared as lithe and smooth and sensuous as a panther. Having lost weight, he was lean and beautiful – he had never looked better.

Elvis himself was terrified, fearing failure. He worried most about the informal talking he was supposed to do during the jam session – telling stories without a script. He had progressed far beyond the tendency to mumble, but he was still shy about speaking up. 'What if nobody likes me?' Elvis kept asking. He almost backed out at the last minute, but he met the challenge, drawing on his self-effacing charm to hide his fear. He was filmed sitting in a sort of boxing ring, laughing and bantering with Scotty and D. J. and a couple of others. You could still see the deference, the down-look. Elvis played with his image. He laughed at it. His modesty was seductive, winning. He made fun of his trademark lip curl. He sang a ballad, 'Are You Lonesome Tonight?', and fooled around with a mock Ink Spots-style recitation. The banter and camaraderie, however nervous Elvis was, weren't stilted or programmed, but natural and real.

Standing in the leather suit in the small arena, he performed a medley of his hits: a fierce 'Heartbreak Hotel', 'Hound Dog', 'All Shook Up'. He sang with stunning control and energy. All his talent – suppressed so long during his Hollywood years – came surging back, full force. He was a revelation. Long-legged, with long-toed motorcycle boots, he stood in that rocking posture of the labourer, legs forming an arch, as if he were ready to swing an axe to fell an oak. He performed old songs like 'Lawdy Miss Clawdy' and 'That's All Right (Mama)' while sitting down, his heebie-jeebie legs still working. But now he seemed sleek, sophisticated, polished, his raw urgency under control. In part, it was illusion – Elvis the pro, putting on his Elvis act. But in part, what the audience saw was the truth – Elvis returning to his true vocation, revelling in it, and reclaiming a more deeply felt sense of himself. In any event, it was mesmerizing. Elvis's energy, masked by his recent dreadful movies, burst forth. He seemed grown now, sexually provocative in an adult way. The sixties may have meant the sexual revolution, with rock music exploding and exploring sexual freedom, but none of the rock groups of the sixties exuded sensuality as Elvis did in this 1968 show. One doesn't recall the Jefferson Airplane, Herman's Hermits, Janis Joplin, the Grateful Dead, or even the Beatles as being especially sexy. For all the raunchiness of the Rolling Stones, Mick Jagger's moves were so peculiar that Elvis found him hilarious. Certainly Mick was no Adonis.

During rehearsals for the special, Billy Goldenberg, the arranger, was surprised to find Elvis one day picking out Beethoven's *Moonlight* Sonata on the piano. The two began working on it together every night, enjoying the quiet diversion into a rich, sophisticated music. Then one night two or three of Elvis's guys interrupted them and spoiled the mood with a snide putdown of classical music. Goldenberg said that Elvis immediately stopped playing, 'as if some strange, dark shadow had come over the place'. Elvis was embarrassed that his guys had seen him flirting with high-tone, uptown art – art that violated their shared tastes. The Beatles had crossed that line, but Elvis was still afraid of being laughed at if he jumped into an unfamiliar highbrow domain.

The show was taped in the summer of 1968, and Martin Luther King had been killed in Memphis. Elvis, who was deeply affected by what had happened in his own town, realized that it was time to abandon frivolous songs and sing what he believed and felt. The closing number of the show, 'If I Can Dream', was written for Elvis specifically to express his dreams of freedom and equality. The song seemed to echo King's famous 'I Have a Dream' speech.

The show, which became known informally as 'The Comeback Special', aired on NBC in December 1968, and was a huge surprise success – as if the Elvis of 1956 had been turned loose again. But the changing times made him seem less of an anomaly at this later date. In the midst of war, social turmoil, and assassinations, Elvis was a welcome old friend, not an assault on decency. The *New York Times* changed its tune from 'vulgar' (1956) to 'charismatic'. The single 'If I Can Dream' became Elvis's biggest hit in years.

Early in 1969, genuinely invigorated by making good music again, Elvis went into American Studio in Memphis, which had become the centre of soul music. There, back on his home turf, he was challenged musically more than he had been at any time since Sam Phillips invited him into Sun Studio. At American, with studio head Chips Moman and with the producer from Nashville, Felton Jarvis, Elvis recorded some of his best music of the decade – 'Suspicious Minds', 'Long Black Limousine', 'Kentucky Rain', 'I Can't Stop Loving You', and numerous others. He brought a new depth of feeling and a heightened artistry to these innovative new recordings. He had never worked with such enthusiasm. The songs from the American sessions captured the new musical directions Elvis had been thinking about for some time, incorporating elements of contemporary country, gospel, soul, and blues into his style. He immersed himself in the new songs with a passion and depth that he hadn't expressed since he recorded his spiritual album *How Great Thou Art* in 1966. Elvis the artist emerged again with confidence in his musical instincts. Although he hesitated at first, he even risked doing a kind of song he had usually avoided – a song with a political overtone. 'If I Can Dream' had paved the way for 'In the Ghetto', a socially aware song more suited to the times than what Elvis had been recording. Peter Guralnick calls 'In the Ghetto', 'Suspicious Minds', and 'Only the Strong Survive' 'a new hybrid style, a cross between "Old Shep" and contemporary soul, in which Elvis can fully believe'. This was the direction Elvis wanted, songs he could pour his heart into, songs that would let him use his voice sincerely and completely. Now he could give full rein to the sounds from his accumulated experience, going back to earliest childhood – the desolate moans, as well as shouts of celebration and exuberance, that came from the downtrodden people around him. Even if Elvis didn't remember what he heard at Parchman Farm, or even if his father never repeated the chants, he did hear sounds of the blues everywhere around him. He grew up in Mississippi, after all. Elvis would have heard sundown field hollers – the long-drawn-out moans of liberation at the end of the workday – right in East Tupelo. The sounds would have carried from the nearby fields around, and from the neighbourhood of Shake Rag. The sounds of the blues – levee-camp moans, juke-joint blues, work chants – were in the air. Elvis absorbed them deep into his soul. The sounds he sang at the end of the sixties came out of his own life – the fight against poverty, the struggle to become somebody, the humiliations suffered by the country person, the loss of his mother, the shame of his father's Parchman sentence. One of the songs Elvis recorded in the Memphis sessions was 'I Washed My Hands in Muddy Water', a poignant, personal story-song about the sins of the father visited upon the son – a story about crime and prison. But the public did not know how personal this was.

Elvis knew he wanted to perform live again. At the conclusion of the taping of the TV special back in the summer, he had told the Colonel he wanted to tour again. The Colonel was making plans. Now, after slogging through his final movie commitment, *Change of Habit*, Elvis was ready.

LAS VEGAS

FOLLOWING 'THE COMEBACK Special', Elvis went on to refashion himself in a way that would exalt him into mythic status. Elvis Presley's second apotheosis was the culmination of his ambition – from Tupelo to Memphis, from Lansky's to Las Vegas. In bringing his hubba-hubba vibrato to Las Vegas, he challenged the showbiz establishment there, and he created the ultimate Elvis in a dazzling stage show that unified his diverse musical passions.

Not yet prepared to send Elvis out on a road tour, Colonel Parker arranged for a long engagement in Las Vegas to lay the foundation. Perhaps the Colonel already had roulette wheels turning in his mind – he later developed a gambling habit – and figured it would be to his advantage to place Elvis in Las Vegas. And he could get maximum income with least exposure for Elvis there. Even though Vegas was hardly more wholesome or less phoney than Hollywood, Elvis was eager to play a glitzy showroom in Sin City. To him, it was the pinnacle of show business, the sacred territory of great performers like Frank Sinatra and Dean Martin, Elvis's heroes. To succeed there would give Elvis his vindication – acceptance by the big dudes and classy dames who had once derided him.

Back in 1956, the Colonel had booked Elvis in Las Vegas for two weeks, but the high rollers and cocktail-lounge lizards weren't ready for the Hillbilly Cat, as he was often called then. Elvis was miserable. 'After that first night I went outside and just walked around in the dark,' he said. 'It was awful.' But he enjoyed meeting Liberace and Johnnie Ray, and he loved the beguiling atmosphere of the place. And after seeing Freddie Bell and the Bellboys do their interpretation of 'Hound Dog', he was prompted to do his own sexy version on *The Milton Berle Show* – the performance that started the storm of controversy for Elvis.

Remembering 1956 when he bombed in Vegas, Elvis was eager to come full circle, but he was nervous as he headed for Nevada in July 1969. However, he was armed with a new confidence in his art. Now Elvis was no longer a threat to America's youth, and he had material that would reach a mature audience. In fact, he had fans the world over who would be loyal, no matter what he did musically. But Elvis persisted in his fear of disappointing them. Consequently, he worked wholeheartedly, auditioning musicians and back-up vocalists, rehearsing tirelessly.

The show Elvis created, and which evolved throughout the remainder of his life, was an astonishing piece of show business. Elvis had been inspired by the way Steve Binder, producer of 'The Comeback Special', covered the different stages of Elvis's career through his musical styles – the country singer, the wild guitar man, the gospel singer, and the contemporary soul singer. Elvis incorporated these themes into his new show, pulling together all the types of music he loved.

In July 1969, the astronauts went to the moon. Elvis went to Las Vegas. He opened to a celebrity audience in the new International Hotel's showroom, which seated two thousand. It was a grandiose, ornate setting, with chandeliers and a gold curtain. Elvis had probably never been more nervous. But as soon as he lit into 'Blue Suede Shoes' he was an instant hit. It was a night unparalleled for excitement in Las Vegas. His energy was phenomenal; the undisciplined wiggling of the fifties now had style and force. The jiggling left leg was more subtle and suggestive. Elvis held the audience on every beat, sensing where to take it, the joy of freedom rising from the sweat of his labour. He still held the wide-legged stance, but the guitar was only a prop – light, an expendable burden. Thin and handsome in a black karate-style Cossack outfit with a high collar and a neckerchief, Elvis let loose. He did zany monologues. He rolled around onstage. He told stories, full of humour and self-mockery and the wordplay he was so fond of. The love of performing came back to him. He was a master showman. Now he had the power. He was – by God – *Elvis*!

He said to the audience, 'Good evening, ladies and gentlemen. Welcome to the big, freaky International Hotel, with these weirdo dolls on the walls and those little funky angels on the ceiling, and man, you ain't seen nothing until you've seen a funky angel. Before the evening's out I'm sure I will have made a complete and utter fool of myself – but I hope you get a kick out of watching.'

As he told his life story, he joked about his rise to fame. People in New York were saying, 'Get him, get him, hot damn, he's just out of the trees.' He made fun of *The Steve Allen Show*, where he had sung to the basset hound. ('The dog is peeing, and I didn't know it.')

The audience at opening night was thunderstruck. Everyone who saw Elvis perform reported that he was unbelievably exciting to watch. Elvis's energy, his flair for dramatics, his wholehearted renditions of soul songs, even his athletics – somersaults and cartwheels – were amazing. Priscilla wrote in her book, 'Elvis exuded a maleness about him, a proudness that you only see in an animal. On the stage he'd have this look, you know, prowling back and forth, pacing like a tiger, and you look and you say, "My god, is this the person that I–?" It was difficult to attach who he was to this person onstage. It was incredible.' Priscilla, who had known him for ten years, had never really seen him perform before, except at the taping of 'The Comeback Special'.

After the show, there occurred possibly the only recorded instance of secretive, cryptic Colonel Parker with tears in his eyes, hugging his boy. (The Colonel had not failed to set up his souvenir booth in the lobby.) Elvis told the press, 'I've always wanted to perform on the stage again for the last nine years, and it's been building up inside of me since 1965 until the strain became intolerable. ... I don't think I could have left it much longer.'

The four-week engagement at the International was the most successful act in Las Vegas history, grossing a million and a half dollars and resulting in an agreement for Elvis to perform two four-week stints per year in Vegas.

In 'The Comeback Special', the gospel segment had allowed Elvis to indulge himself in the form he loved best. He appeared in a pulpit with the Blossoms, a trio of black gospel singers dressed in white, and they sang 'Where Could I Go But to the Lord' and 'Up Above My Head'. Elvis took the gospel sound and ran with it to Las Vegas. He hired the Sweet Inspirations (a soul group) and the Imperials (a white gospel quartet). The Imperials were later replaced by the Stamps, with J. D. Sumner, who had been with the Blackwood Brothers when the teenage Elvis attended their all-night singings. These groups harmonized and filled in the background, to create the large sound Elvis wanted. In Las Vegas, after the shows, guests typically congregated in Elvis's suite, and often he would stay up all night, singing gospel songs with the Imperials or with other entertainers who stopped by. Elvis had been practising a version of this behaviour all his life – singing at church, at home with his parents, at Graceland with his friends.

As his new show evolved in the early years, he let rip with the deepest emotions he could express. He dug down into his life and laid it out before him. 'I Can't Stop Loving You', 'Can't Help Falling in Love', the bluesy 'Reconsider Baby', 'Memories', 'The Wonder of You', 'Walk a Mile in My Shoes'. He ranged widely over old favourites: 'Love Me Tender', 'Hound Dog', 'Jailhouse Rock'. And he affirmed his rural Southern roots with a narrative song, 'Polk Salad Annie'. (No doubt Gladys had many times cooked 'poke sallet' – green shoots of pokeweed that rural people gathered from the woods in the spring.)

Elvis defied and transcended all categories except himself.

Drawing on all the strains of music that had sustained him through the years, he reached to the bottom of his heart and sang his own blue notes, adding at least forty-five layers of soul, celebration, pain, and pizzazz. A long way from the innocent kid with the guitar making fresh noise at Sun Records and on the *Louisiana Hayride*, he was now Elvis the King in his glory. From 1970 to 1973, he perfected his stage act, pouring more energy into a performance than seemed humanly possible.

As Elvis's show evolved through the early seventies, his costumes began to bear the lavish, dramatic look forever associated with him. His comic-book hero from childhood, Captain Marvel, was reincarnated in a gem-studded jump-suit with a splendid bejewelled cape. The design, by Bill Belew, grew out of seventies fashion – leisure suits, bell-bottoms – and links back to the aspirations of country musicians, who sported the flash of rhinestones in their fancy Western-style outfits. But Elvis's costume outdid all the go-to-the-*Opry* duds of Nashville. In his super-suit, Elvis could be confident of his unique role.

At Madison Square Garden in New York on 10 June, 1972, he is at his peak. It is an extravaganza, with so many voices backing him it is like some bedazzled choir from heaven – two vocal groups and a rock band, all fronting an orchestra. The show begins with *Also Sprach Zarathustra*, known as the theme from *2001: A Space Odyssey*. Elvis sweeps majestically onto the stage in one of his extravagant high-collared outfits, his magic guitar held like an M-16 rifle athwart his middle. After kneeling to touch and kiss the women bobbing at the footlights, he rises and launches into 'That's All Right', a song that has lost its strangeness and become instead a celebration of Elvis the Phenomenon. He discards the guitar early in the show, letting his body become instrument and art. He sings a few of his biggest hits from the fifties and alternates some of the power ballads like 'The Impossible Dream' with upbeat, shook-up rockers. 'American Trilogy' is one of his grand show-stoppers: a medley of 'Dixie', 'Battle Hymn of the Republic', and 'All My Trials, Lord' – sort of corny and bombastic, but majestically rendered and Elvis at his most sincere. He was widely praised for his performance, and *The New Yorker* lauded his professionalism. The *New York Times* compared him to Joe DiMaggio, 'a champion, the only one in his class'.

In 1973, *Aloha from Hawaii*, the televised concert beamed around the world by satellite to an estimated one and a half billion people, Elvis appears in all his splendour. At the end of the show, when he spreads out his American Eagle cape, with the full stretched wings of the eagle studded on the back, he becomes a god figure.

His passion for music and his command of his art still prevailed in the studio as well as on the stage. After 'The Comeback Special', Elvis, freed from the constraints of movie music, vowed never again to record a song that he didn't feel. He often reached back to songs from the fifties that he had admired, like 'Faded Love' and 'I Really Don't Want to Know'. More important, he threw himself into the big-hearted soul ballads he loved, like 'I've Lost You' and 'Twenty Days and Twenty Nights'. But audiences were finding his stage performances more thrilling than they did his new recordings.

For the first couple of years, his Vegas engagements rejuvenated him. But there was a falseness about his relationship to Sin City. From the start of his career, Elvis had been attracted to the gambling mecca, but not for the gambling. For him, the glitter of Las Vegas meant adolescent fun. He wanted to stay up late so he wouldn't have nightmares; he wanted the flashing bright lights because he wanted artifice, not the sun. His desires were innocent. But Vegas was where the ultimate game operated at the highest stakes.

CAPTAIN MARVEL GOES TO WASHINGTON

ELVIS HAD ONCE been invited to perform for President Nixon at the White House, but the Colonel wouldn't permit him to go because the White House did not pay invited performers. Let the President pay like anybody else, the Colonel responded.

In December 1970, Elvis decided to go to the White House on his own. Of all the Elvis capers on record, his visit to President Richard Nixon has to be among the strangest.

By then, Elvis had established his base in Las Vegas, and he had taken the show on the road for a brief, wildly successful run. The old magic had been rekindled, and the fans were in a new frenzy. In the fringed and belted outfits inspired by his passion for karate, Elvis felt invincible on stage. But offstage, he lived in a different state of urgency. Now he was a husband and a father; Lisa Marie was born in Memphis on 1 February, 1968. Although his life had changed positively with marriage and the revitalization of his career, he was far from settled. He was perturbed by the assassinations, Woodstock, anti-war protesters, and the lack of respect for authority. He was troubled by drug use among young people, but he would never admit that his own use of prescription drugs was in the same realm. The Charles Manson murders in California had unnerved him, and he had received death threats in Las Vegas. He grew paranoid and obsessed with protecting himself. He inherited his mother's deep dread. If Gladys had lived, she would surely have gone insane with worry after Elvis returned to live performing. His fears drove him to an obsession with guns. He had always loved uniforms and had wanted to be a cop. Since he depended on police-men to such an extent for security wherever he went, he spent a lot of time with them. He admired authority and had the chance to wear a cop uniform on several occasions when he was made an honorary policeman. He developed fantasies of carrying out drug raids and arrests. He made friends with policemen in various cities, and he had a large collection of badges they had given him. He also had a growing collection of guns. Ultimately, he felt he had a mission to fight the drug culture, which was infiltrating the music world. To this end, he decided he needed a badge from the Bureau of Narcotics and Dangerous Drugs. He wanted to be a special agent for the federal government.

Priscilla, almost from the beginning of their marriage, had watched it disintegrate as Elvis insisted on continuing many of his bachelor habits. His preoccupation with his work had estranged them, and his extreme behaviour – obsessions, whims, pills, and infidelities – were beyond her coping. She observed how much Elvis needed to perform; it set him at ease, and he couldn't be still otherwise. In Las Vegas, he felt so buoyed by his performances – his nervous system still leaping from the amphetamines he took before the show – that afterwards he held court for hours in his seven-room luxury penthouse suite at the hotel. Just as Elvis felt a genuine need to perform for his fans, he also needed to splurge on gifts for friends and family. But his spending in late 1970 grew alarming to Priscilla and Vernon, who eventually confronted him over it. (Rarely did anyone confront Elvis over anything.) He was out of control, they told him. For instance, after one of his sprees he shouldn't be trying to placate his father by buying him a Mercedes. Vernon feared a replay of the Circle G ranch fiasco. Elvis had been buying cars and houses willy-nilly for people, paying for weddings, buying twenty thousand dollars' worth of guns at one haul. While shopping, he bought gifts for strangers.

That December, when Priscilla and Vernon challenged him, Elvis reacted with disbelief. Then he disappeared. For the first time since 1956 he took off on his own. He simply left home and went to the airport by himself. He flew on a commercial flight to Washington, intending to visit a woman with whom he had been having an affair. He apparently had nothing with him except a little cardboard box of toiletries. Little is known about that leg of the journey – how did he pay his way, how did he know what to do? Priscilla said he didn't even know his own telephone number and never carried cash. Unable to locate the woman because he'd lost her telephone number, he flew from Washington to Dallas, where he called one of his guys, Jerry Schilling, and asked him to meet him in Los Angeles with some clothing. Once there, Elvis decided to fly back to Washington with Jerry, who insisted on getting Sonny West, another of the guys, to meet them in

Washington, to help with security. While on the plane, Elvis took a notion to write a letter on American Airlines stationery to President Nixon. In the letter, Elvis asked to be made a Federal Agent at Large, and he offered to help Nixon in the war on drugs. Young people looked up to him, he said.

Elvis wrote Nixon, 'The drug culture, the hippie elements, the SDS, Black Panthers, etc. do *not* consider me as their enemy or as they call it The Establishment. *I call it America and* I love it.' Elvis told the President he had been nominated by the Junior Chamber of Commerce as 'one of America's Ten Most Outstanding Young Men', and he enclosed a 'short autobiography about myself'. In a postscript, Elvis mentioned that he had a gift for the President.

It was an unusual match, but Elvis actually had much in common with Richard Nixon. Both lived an insulated existence, protected by their minions. Nixon had Haldeman and Ehrlichman; Elvis had the Memphis Mafia. Nixon once surrounded the White House with a wall of buses to protect himself from protesters; Colonel Parker metaphorically circled his covered wagons around Elvis.

Elvis delivered his letter at the White House gate at the crack of dawn. He and Jerry returned to their hotel, and later in the morning Elvis went to the Bureau of Narcotics and Dangerous Drugs, but he had no luck getting the badge from an official there. Meanwhile, Nixon's people jumped at this political opportunity for the President to ingratiate himself with millions of Elvis fans and quickly prepared memos for Nixon. By 12:30, Elvis was in the Oval Office, playing mind games with President Richard Nixon. The meeting has been recounted in detail by Egil Krogh, who was an aide to the

President at the time, and Sonny West has also published his memories.

Elvis, enjoying a golden opportunity for playing dress-up, arrived in full Elvis regalia: amber-tinted aviator sunglasses, dark pants, a purple velvet V-necked tunic, a high-collared white shirt, a gold belt with a buckle shield the size of a tray, a pendant on a gold rope, and his Tree of Life necklace with all his guys' names engraved on the branches. The whole outfit culminated in a splendid military-style jacket worn like a cape – part pea jacket (with brass buttons), part Batman, and part Captain Marvel. He was wearing make-up, and he almost surely was stoned.

Speechless with awe for the first thirty seconds after entering the Oval Office, Elvis was soon doing a snow job on the President. Clearly, Nixon was in a nonplus and thought Elvis peculiar, to say the least. Elvis apparently impressed President Nixon with his sincerity and charm, and the odd pair seemed to hit it off. Nixon was interested in Elvis's offer to help with the administration's anti-drug campaign.

Out of the blue, Elvis warned Nixon about the Beatles, saying they were anti-American. The remark confused Nixon, for the Beatles weren't mentioned in the staff memos, and he may not have been aware that they had promoted LSD and marijuana. These were drugs Elvis had tried, to see what they were like – the same way he had tried the Beatles for one visit at his house. But he didn't mention that now.

'I'm just a poor boy from Tennessee,' Elvis told the President. 'I've gotten a lot from my country. And I'd like to do something to repay for what I've gotten.'

'That will be very helpful,' Nixon said.

'I've been studying Communist brainwashing for over ten years now, and the drug culture, too,' Elvis told the President. He offered his services in communicating with young people through his work. 'I can go right into a group of hippies and young people and be accepted,' he said. 'This can be real helpful.'

He had brought along some of his badge collection, in leather cases, to show the President. With his manipulative charm, Elvis soon had Nixon spontaneously promising the coveted BNDD badge. Elvis was so overcome with joy that he hugged the President, a gesture as startling to Nixon as anything hippies might have said to him. (Priscilla later claimed that Elvis wanted that badge simply so that he could legally carry all the prescription drugs he finagled into his possession and so that he and the Memphis Mafia could carry guns.)

Richard Nixon said, 'You dress kind of strange, don't you?'

Elvis said, 'You have your show and I have mine.'

Nixon opened a desk drawer to find presidential tie clasps to give the guys for souvenirs. By then Sonny West and Jerry Schilling had been ushered into the Oval Office, at Elvis's instigation. Emboldened by his new intimacy with the Commander in Chief, Elvis started rummaging in Nixon's drawer, in search of more souvenirs. 'Remember, Mr President, they've got wives,' he said. He found some pins with the presidential seal for them, and Nixon loaded the three men with souvenirs.

When Elvis went home from Washington, exultant about meeting the President and acquiring the badge, he splurged some more on Christmas gifts, including four Mercedes.

He had been forced to leave his gift for the President at the security gate. It was a handgun with seven silver bullets – a collectors' World War II Colt .45 that had seen battle in several places in Europe and Africa. But later that month Elvis somehow managed to tour the FBI wearing two guns.

With incidents like this, people around him worried that Elvis was losing his grip on reality. By the time he went to Washington, propelled by anger and disbelief that his family would try to talk sense to him, his drug use had increased. The energy required for performing was pushing him deeper into dependence on uppers, downers, and pain relievers. Elvis feared hard drugs, but he still believed his prescription pills were legitimate, safe, and necessary.

Perhaps in going to the White House for a narc badge, Elvis was pulling off a brilliant prank. Perhaps the paradox of the rock rebel and the right-wing, gun-toting vigilante wasn't lost on him. We can also easily conclude that he was delusional from medication he was taking. Elvis, with his passive nature, would not normally have dreamed of muscling his way into the White House. But the drug-enhanced Elvis, mega-star and King, could roam the world with confidence and impunity. As the caped avenger Elvis seemed insuperable. He could not simply believe in himself; he had to create an alternate Elvis who could do things he could not. The memory of the missing twin was still lodged in his psyche.

With several law-enforcement badges and a black belt in karate, he wanted to join forces with Richard Nixon and J. Edgar Hoover to straighten out the world. All he needed was a badge. In his Captain Marvel cape he could strike terror and awe into people. He could command lightning bolts.

LOST

THE SPECIAL-AGENT badge extended Elvis's sense of authority even further. He loved sporting the badge, along with his other police badges. As a narc cop, he felt he was above the law. Sounding his siren and flashing the blue light on his car, he would sometimes pull over people for speeding. In Washington, DC, in January 1971, his badge still fresh, he ordered his limousine to stop at an accident scene so he could offer assistance. A stunned policeman was agog, and an injured woman, lying on the front seat of her car, gaped in shock at the sight of Elvis and his badge. Elvis loved acting out his childhood fantasy of cops and robbers. At home he had a growing arsenal of guns and a wardrobe of Superfly private-eye outfits. Several years after he got his badge, he was passing by a gas station when he saw two men assaulting a station attendant. Elvis stopped, bounded out of his limo, and broke up the fight with some karate moves. The participants were so amazed to see Elvis Presley that they stopped fighting, and Elvis posed for pictures with them.

Soon after the visit to Nixon, Elvis was best man at Sonny

West's wedding in Memphis. Elvis, feeling he had to protect himself and watch out for perps and psychos, carried five guns in his bell-bottomed fur-cloth suit. The others had to talk him out of taking his fifteen-inch police flashlight to the altar. Later, he demanded that everyone leave the reception and go to Graceland instead; once there, he decided they should all – including the bride and groom, on their wedding night – go to the Memphian Theatre to watch movies with him. Elvis insisted on being the centre of any event.

This wasn't the Elvis everyone had loved – the good boy who treated people right. He had changed. Priscilla said Elvis 'bought his own image'. It is too simple to say he got the big head, got above his raising. It's too simple, too, to blame everything on his prescription pills. In part, Elvis's behaviour seems to have been the logical outcome for a man who lived his adult life as a child whose every whim and fantasy could be realized. Elvis saw no contradiction between his obsession with guns and his quest for spiritual growth, his selfish tantrums and his humble faith. He could still function in daily life; he was still charming and generous, not always paranoid or delirious from drugs. But he remained basically insecure, doubtful of his own worth. Thus, he was exceptionally proud of being chosen by the national Junior Chamber of Commerce as one of the Ten Outstanding Young Men in America. Significantly, the award ceremony was held in Memphis. As he often did, Elvis went overboard, inviting everyone at the Jaycees gathering to Graceland for cocktails and then hosting a Chateaubriand dinner at a restaurant. When he accepted his award, he gave an eloquent speech, saying, 'When I was a child, ladies and gentlemen, I was a dreamer. I read comic books, and I was the hero of the comic book. I saw movies, and I was the hero in the movie. So every dream that I ever dreamed has come true a hundred times.' Elvis was so proud of his trophy, a touching-hands sculpture, that he carried it with him on all his travels for the rest of his life.

As he told the Jaycees, Elvis had fulfilled his boyish fantasies more completely than he could have dared hope. He had become a music superstar, then a movie star; after he faded, he staged a triumphal comeback. But the wild swirl of super-celebrity made it harder and harder for Elvis to understand his life, to grow as an artist or as a person. He didn't live in the world of everyday normality. He lived in Elvisland. Eventually he could not do the simplest things for himself; he could not adjust the picture on the TV set but had to telephone his dad in the middle of the night to come in and fiddle with the knob. When he took out one of the little cigars he was fond of, a dozen lighters would flash forward to light it for him. If no one offered such assistance, Elvis might lose his temper. At such moments, Elvis's dark doppelgänger seemed to emerge – angry, impetuous, violent, frightening. Everyone in his employ feared these hot-headed outbursts, and they feared being ousted. The cooks indulged him with comfort food. The members of the Memphis Mafia continued to make it possible for Elvis to do whatever he wanted. They provided companionship, and they were forever ready to handle any spontaneous errands and jobs that came up. If Elvis wanted to buy a Mercedes in the middle of the night, somebody figured out how it could be done. Sometimes Elvis included a jeweller in his entourage when he toured, with a stock of baubles from the jewellery store, so that if he got into a gift-buying mood he would have some selections available in an instant. As the King, he felt he deserved to live lavishly. But his pattern of binges and bouts of generosity kept him literally enslaved. Just as when he was locked into his movie contracts, Elvis was stuck in a new cycle of working to earn more and more money to keep up his lifestyle.

He was nervous, his leg often bobbing uncontrollably, even when he sat quietly at home. He was distracted, propelled by whims and secret urges and strange desires.

Priscilla couldn't deal with his increasingly out-of-control behaviour. He was treating her badly – staying away from home for several weeks at a time, and stipulating that she could come to Las Vegas only for the openings and closings of the engagements. It was like the Hollywood years, before they married, when he expected her to wait patiently at Graceland for him while he wooed his leading ladies. Priscilla had been a child when she fell in love with Elvis. Growing up at Graceland, she had every hope of being married to him in a romantic, fulfilling way. But Elvis, although he always claimed to love her deeply, never treated her as an equal, grown-up partner. He even turned away from her sexually after their daughter was born, having always found sex and motherhood incompatible notions. Eventually Priscilla began to gain some independence. In 1972, seeing that Elvis was becoming hopeless to deal with, she left him – for another man, her karate instructor. Elvis was crushed. Losing Priscilla was a major blow to his ego. In a fit of rage, he ordered Red West to hire a hit man to kill

Priscilla's boyfriend. It took some time for Elvis to be talked out of the idea, so great was his hurt and anger.

Even before the divorce in 1973, Elvis reached out to various women for love and protection; he needed constant love and maternal care. He needed his entourage, his large circle of admirers. He still believed that without his fans, he would be a common labourer. Discounting to a great extent his own part in his success – his talent and ambition and hard work – and crediting the fans for such an enormous gift, he was subservient to his image, eternally obligated. But harbouring his own doubts about himself, he slid towards depression.

And he needed more drugs – not only the uppers, but the downers and painkillers he had begun to use even more frequently. He had ways of acquiring medicines from various doctors. He had studied the *Physicians' Desk Reference* and knew how to pick drugs he wanted to try; with his knowledge of the drugs he could contrive symptoms and wheedle doctors into prescribing whatever he wanted. On one occasion, he went to a pharmacist's house on a Sunday, when the drugstore was closed, and asked for certain drugs. The pharmacist was so astonished to find Elvis Presley at his door that he complied.

Vernon Presley stood on the sidelines of his son's desperate antics. 'Oh, Lordy!' It is worth noting how Elvis's father turned out – the man who was impoverished for the first forty years of his life, then was lifted into a wacky, home-grown jet-set life. Although his Depression background made him tight with money, he settled willingly into affluence, complete with expensive suits and jewellery, and tried to assert some authority and dignity while living off his son's earnings. Elvis trusted Vernon to be his personal financial manager, because he knew his parsimonious father was suspicious of everyone, so he would be protective. And Vernon always defended Elvis. But this role was also what a young boy expects from his father – a caretaker and protector. It was up to Vernon to pay the bills, to lament and fight his son's indulgences, to lay down the law with employees. In some ways, he remained a man with simple habits. He sometimes ate meat-and-three at the Piccadilly Cafeteria near Graceland, and in the early years he mowed the Graceland grounds and kept the vehicles running – perhaps for lack of anything else to do. He loved tinkering with old cars. He tried to run an automobile dealership but lost money. He had a non-speaking part in one of Elvis's movies. He was unfaithful to his second wife, Dee, and eventually they divorced. He lived in a house on a street behind Graceland – furnished in a flamboyant style similar to that of Graceland. His house had a small tiled pool in the bedroom. He had insomnia and heart trouble. And he drank.

Vernon's job was to keep Graceland running and stave off bankruptcy. His fear of a return to poverty kept him lashed to Colonel Parker.

A major key to Elvis's rise and fall was the Presleys' allegiance to Colonel Parker. The provincial, unsophisticated thinking of Elvis and his father kept them in the Colonel's clutches throughout, even though a number of times Elvis struggled to free himself. By trusting a man they believed was a Southerner, whom they could relate to and admire for his clever strategies, they doomed themselves to the man's manipulations. The Colonel was successful, cranking out the merchandise and earning top dollar. The movies, the ground-breaking music, Elvis lunch boxes – all just merchandise, all equally valid in the Colonel's world. He evaluated everything by its price tag, or by the profit he could wring from it. He helped Elvis grow rich, but he also boxed Elvis into a mercenary, essentially mean-spirited partnership. Ideally, Elvis's manager would have understood his artistic vision and – as an older, wiser man – would have helped him to grow. The Colonel couldn't do this. Neither could Vernon. So Elvis was left undirected, unguided, except by his own blazing hopes and dreams.

There is a strain of tawdriness in Elvis's story, growing out of his poverty and the materialistic values it fostered. A hungry state of mind had led the Presleys to the Colonel – a man who came from a cheap, discount world. He was a man who gave waitresses calendars for tips and connived to stockpile free food from hotels. His office was crazily set up like a travelling-show cook tent, with oilcloth-covered tables. Company executives found him perplexing to deal with. He did business in arcane ways, by investing the concept of loyalty with mystery, by hiding his lack of real sophistication with obfuscating babble.

In 1973, the Colonel agreed to sell Elvis's back catalogue, with forfeiture of royalties, to RCA Victor for $5.4 million cash up front. And he drew up a new contract between himself and Elvis for a fifty-fifty split on new earnings from future recordings. Along with a new RCA recording contract and a few side deals, the Colonel managed to come out ahead of Elvis. Later, in 1976, the Colonel revised his deal with Elvis on the tour profits – a fifty-fifty split instead of two-thirds for Elvis.

Throughout his career, Elvis complained about the Colonel's power over him, but he allowed it. Their relationship was symbiotic. In fact, Elvis was the Colonel's whole life. There was an affectionate bond between them, a pairing characterized by loyalty and trust – that is, Elvis not asking questions and the Colonel not revealing more than necessary. But finally, in 1973, Elvis's growing frustrations erupted in a showdown. Onstage at the Hilton (formerly the International) in Las Vegas, Elvis lashed out at the hotel for firing a waiter he liked. After the show, the Colonel blew up at Elvis, railing over his unprofessional stage manner. So Elvis fired him. The Colonel calmly said he would be presenting his bill for expenses and other debts Elvis owed him. The blow-up resulted in a bitter estrangement for two weeks. The Colonel's bill turned out to be two million dollars, and Elvis and Vernon backtracked. They did not realize that any number of managers might have paid them two million dollars – or more – just for the chance to handle Elvis. The Colonel had them buffaloed.

The Colonel cannot be wholly blamed; he was doing what he knew how to do, what Elvis hired him to do. But his influence nonetheless was pernicious. Elvis allowed himself to be handled by a man who had no conception of artistic merit or challenge. They had once made a fine team. The Colonel had packaged the products of Elvis's talent so successfully that Elvis became world-famous. The Colonel and Elvis had made a pact, and Elvis stuck to his end of the bargain – for better, at first, and then increasingly for worse.

In Las Vegas, while Elvis retreated to his penthouse suite, entertaining streams of visitors and encircled by his protectors, the Colonel hit the gaming tables. More than ever, the Colonel needed his boy to earn, so that he could play. Elvis, too, needed to keep working, to keep up with the rate he was spending. Dutifully, Elvis continued touring at the demanding pace set by the Colonel – twenty or thirty one-nighters at a stretch. And each engagement in Vegas meant two shows a day, seven days a week, for a month. Although he earned even more from performances than he had from the movies, Elvis still felt compelled to keep up the schedule so that he could make the payroll of all the people who depended on him. The tour alone required thirty-nine people. He couldn't just quit, although it was an idea he still sometimes entertained even as he splurged on gifts. As the tours progressed through the decade of the seventies, he became bored with the show he had created. He grew to hate Las Vegas. His performances became strange and disjointed. And when Elvis became bored with performing, he was lost.

THE END OF
LONELY STREET

ELVIS NEVER STOPPED being amazed at himself – amazed at the phenomenon of Elvis the King. One day in the seventies he entered a pet shop, and all the dogs leaped in their cages, clamouring for attention. 'Yes, it's me, Elvis Presley,' Elvis joked. It was, in fact, a symbolic moment. For nearly twenty years, from his ascendancy in 1956, fans and hangers-on had clustered around him with dog-like devotion, eager to do anything for him, begging to be chosen, hinting for favours, craving attention.

Yet Elvis was alone. No one else around him had been through what he had. He had no peers, no soulmates, no true confidants. He had found the perfect drug in his youth, being the King, and to sustain that transcendent experience he needed more and more affirmation. He needed fortifying chemicals to help him stay on his emotional mountaintop, or alternately to shut down to find momentary release. But he couldn't give up that original fabulous apotheosis, when he became a god on earth. He was addicted to being Elvis.

Ironically, to a great extent, what preyed on him and

alienated him in later years was precisely the way people lionized him. Their hero worship distorted his sense of himself. After all, he wanted to be the Elvis they fantasized, too. Most people wanted a bit of stardust from him, plus maybe some cash or a Cadillac if they were lucky. And Elvis tried to give people what they wanted. On one occasion, in 1975, a country singer with a couple of hit songs visited Elvis and kept hinting for Elvis to buy him a tour bus. Elvis was annoyed, recognizing how he was being manipulated, but he gave in and bought the guy the bus.

The greediness of some of his relatives especially distressed him. They were outspoken with their demands, fixing him with their hungry eyes. Even though he provided some of them with a home at Graceland, they kept embarrassing him. On board the *Lisa Marie*, the Convair 880 jet Elvis had bought for his tours, his drunken Aunt Delta pulled a gun from her purse and threatened to shoot one of the bodyguards. When they arrived back at Graceland, Elvis was still so enraged that he threatened to throw her out on the street, but then realized she had nowhere to go. And she was family. Even though Elvis had remained loyal to his kin, his country heritage was a burden. In one of his last recording sessions, he prepared to record a song called 'Country Bumpkin', but the next day he decided against it. 'I'm no country bumpkin,' he said.

The effort to be what others expected him to be grew harder. At some level, Elvis knew the sun god/Apollo he pretended to be onstage was ludicrous. He had always had the tendency to make fun of his image – and he still threw in those little jocular asides, as if to say, 'Ladies and gentlemen, it's all a ridiculous act.' He would bop out of character momentarily, interrupting even the most serious song, with a self-conscious reference to the Elvis persona. He had done this since junior high, and it had always been part of his charm. The Beatles did the same thing. Bob Dylan also grinned around the edges of his mask. But by now there was a pathos in Elvis's humour as he persisted in poking fun at his own image. He allowed himself to become a joke. Instead of riding with the irony, Elvis sabotaged himself. He was utterly serious about his songs – full-throated, powerhouse songs (like 'The Impossible Dream', 'If I Can Dream', and 'American Trilogy') – but by continually interrupting them with self-deprecating remarks and goofy antics, he drained them of meaning or emotional impact. He undermined his own sincerity. So the audience saw Elvis disintegrate; by insisting on his disbelief in himself as the object of adoration, he seemed to plead with the audience to see through his act – to reject him.

He spent his last few years swathed in loneliness and pain. More than a dozen people were charged with taking care of Elvis, but he always outsmarted them when it came to getting the drugs he wanted. His personal doctor, Dr George Nichopoulos, who accompanied him on tour, used placebos when possible in an attempt to wean him from the drugs. But Elvis managed to find other sources. He used his *Physicians' Desk Reference* like a shopping catalogue, deluding himself into thinking he could control his intake. He horded a private pharmacopoeia. He experimented with many kinds of tranquillizers and painkillers. Ultimately, the only way he could feel whole – feel the way the King should feel – was to pop fifty or more pills a day. His regular prescriptions (not under his own name) at the Walgreen's near Graceland included Placidyl and Demerol. Towards the end of his life, he was also injecting cocaine. And he used several other drugs for various physical ailments. Steroids caused fluid retention, which made him appear heavier than he was. Although he had always been able to keep trim before, he began gaining weight as he took more depressant drugs. The press sensationalized his weight, but in the deep-fried South, his shape was a familiar sight, typical of his age group.

His health was a huge blind spot. Elvis repeated his mother's behaviour: denial of a problem, secrecy about it, refusal to let the hospital do extensive tests, a feeling of shame if the truth were known. Always the extremist, he often ate to excess, sometimes fixating on one food that he would eat exclusively until he tired of it. He craved the Southern specialities he was raised on – fried meat, gravy, crowder peas, greens, mashed potatoes, biscuits, pie. Elvis hired cooks who could cook Southern-style. It was unthinkable to change the food ways of a folk culture. Elvis still cherished memories of the church all-day-singing and dinner-on-the ground – a songfest and feast.

In spite of his declining health, Elvis tried to meet his Las Vegas engagements and keep up the one-nighters – as many as a hundred a year. Onstage, he carried a derringer in his boot for protection and stationed his armed bodyguards nearby, yet he recklessly courted danger in the charged atmosphere. Women flung their underwear to the stage, and they trampled over one another in their frantic rush to get to him. Elvis playfully encouraged their violent hysteria, waving his matador cape and tossing silk scarves to them. They fought each other over the scarves. He teased them, apparently fearing that if he didn't stir up controversy and wild reactions as he had in the fifties, then he truly would have lost his magic.

But gradually, as the drugs overcame him, Elvis cared less about his performances. From 1974 on, he seemed much of the time to have lost his focus. He rambled in lengthy monologues (especially at the informal Hilton showroom in Las Vegas), telling the story of his life, and acting out personal vendettas. He used the Hilton stage one evening to denounce rumours that he was 'strung out' on drugs. He gave a karate demonstration for fifteen minutes in one show. Sometimes he read from one of his spiritual texts. When he got around to singing, he often forgot the lyrics. Sometimes Elvis was half asleep when he went onstage, before his shot of amphetamine kicked in. Once he even fell asleep during a performance. The Colonel cut his schedule from one month to two weeks. After December 1976, he did no Las Vegas shows. During his final engagement in Las Vegas, he wrote some of his pained thoughts on the hotel stationery:

'I have no need for all of this. ... Help me Lord.' 'I don't know who I can talk to any more. Nor to turn to. I only have myself and the Lord. Help me Lord to know the right thing.' 'I feel lost sometimes. Be still and *know I am God*. Feel me within, before you know *I am there*.'

When he was touring, Elvis took more care with his performances than he did in Las Vegas. His real fans were out there, he thought, and he laboured not to disappoint them. He poured his pain into songs that could express his deepest feelings: 'Unchained Melody', 'Bridge over Troubled Water', 'My Way', and the hymn 'How Great Thou Art'. At any time – if the conditions were right, his mood right, his drug level right – Elvis was capable of giving an electrifying performance, as he did on the very last show of his life, in Indianapolis in June 1977, resplendent in his Aztec sun-god jumpsuit.

Elvis was a handful for his caretakers. The Memphis Mafia, treading softly, feared that if they confronted Elvis over his drug problem they would be fired. They knew they still had to be fun, easy for Elvis to be around. They had to defuse his tantrums, turn his childish fits into laughter. Above all, they couldn't humiliate him or embarrass him. Most of the gang dispersed now when Elvis wasn't on the road.

Vernon Presley could not stop his son from destroying himself. He even seemed oblivious to the drug problem. In 1975, from his hospital bed after a heart attack, he angrily accused Elvis of causing the attack. And he said, 'You worried your mama right into the grave.' It was an egregiously insensitive remark that must have ripped Elvis's soul. If Elvis believed it, his self-destruction was inevitable.

Everyone around knew Elvis was in crisis. Still, it was hard for them to believe it or admit it. Linda Thompson, a glamorous Memphis beauty queen with strong maternal instincts, took care of him, even staying with him whenever he was hospitalized. Elvis sustained a long relationship with her after Priscilla left, but eventually Linda was overwhelmed by his neediness and left in late 1976 to reclaim her own life. She realized she could not save Elvis.

Then Elvis found another beautiful woman, Ginger Alden, who was half his age, too young to know about the excitement Elvis had created when he started out. She was bewildered by him, less capable of catering to his whims. Elvis wanted to marry her, but he was unsure of her feelings and found her motives hard to read. Frustrated, he told Larry Geller, 'I'll never know if a woman loves me or "Elvis Presley".' But he clung to her. Something about her reminded him of his mother.

Twice in 1976, RCA sent a mobile unit to Graceland to record Elvis, since he wouldn't go to Nashville, but the sessions fizzled. He was discouraged that he couldn't hit the right notes. Even though he was distracted, he managed a few good songs, including a raw, bleeding version of Roy Hamilton's powerful, soaring interpretation of 'Hurt'. His last recording session took place in the Jungle Room in October 1976. Elvis barely cooperated. He didn't seem to care. But he managed a creditable version of 'Pledging My Love', harking nostalgically back to the sound and style of the fifties.

In the last several months of his life, he wanted fewer people around, and there were fewer outings and frolics. He spent more time alone, sometimes holing up for several days in his bedroom, the windows covered with aluminium foil to keep out the light. Or he rode his horse for hours by himself around the back acreage at Graceland.

When he was awake he often studied his metaphysical and spiritual books. He still hauled a trunk full of books around when he toured. Priscilla's bonfire of his books hadn't eradicated Elvis's devotion to the teachings Larry Geller had introduced him to years before. Elvis still read Kahlil Gibran's *The Prophet*, which June Juanico had given him in 1956. He always kept a copy of it by his bed.

He continued to have nightmares of abandonment. His health deteriorated further. He suffered from glaucoma. During the decade, he had been hospitalized for detox five times, and on a few occasions he almost died. He overdosed three times in one year. But he kept insisting he was in control. He refused to give up drugs or see a psychiatrist. No one could tell him what to do.

During Elvis's last years, his younger cousin Billy Smith, who idolized him, was possibly closer to Elvis than almost anyone except Linda Thompson. It was Billy's father who had been imprisoned with Vernon at Parchman Farm. In 1974, Elvis settled Billy and his wife in a house trailer in the backyard at Graceland, and Billy lived there as Elvis's loyal retainer for the duration. Billy was the person he talked to most during the last two months. They spent hours up in Elvis's lair. Sometimes they just laughed and acted out *Monty Python* routines. And sometimes Elvis played out his paranoid fantasies. But most of the time they just talked.

Elvis was worried about a book being written by Sonny and Red West, the cousins who had been Elvis's loyal friends and bodyguards for years. In 1975, Red had tried to have a heart-to-heart talk with Elvis about how drugs had changed his personality. Elvis seemed to listen thoughtfully, agreeing that the old days had been more fun. But the next day Elvis said adamantly, 'I'm going to do what I want to do and that's the way it is.' The subject was closed. A year later, Vernon, in one of his cost-cutting fits that seemed intended to counterbalance Elvis's spending sprees, fired Red and Red's cousin, Sonny, along with Dave Hebler, another bodyguard, who was newer on the team. Sonny and Red were hurt that Elvis didn't defend them and concluded that he cared nothing for them after all. The three ex-bodyguards decided to write a book about Elvis, exposing his drug problem.

When he learned about the book, Elvis felt enormously betrayed. The code of the Memphis Mafia had been violated. *Elvis, What Happened?* came out the first week of August 1977. According to Billy Smith, Elvis was deeply shaken and depressed by its revelations. His next tour was set to begin in a couple of weeks. He was tormented by the thought that his fans would turn on him. What if they booed? Or called him a dope addict? He worked out various defences – how he needed to take his pills and how his doctor prescribed them. He thought he would introduce his doctor to the audience. Elvis would make a glowing case for himself. But as he agonized, he decided he needed to be straight with his fans. If pressed, he would admit his drug addiction. And he would seek treatment. For once in his life, he wouldn't hide. He worked on a little speech he would give onstage to his fans.

Elvis had been dieting, preparing for the tour, which would begin in Portland, Maine, on 17 August. On 15 August, he didn't eat all day. He went to the dentist that night, and in the wee hours of the next morning, when he couldn't sleep, he summoned Billy and Jo Smith to play racquetball with him and Ginger Alden in the new racquetball building behind the house. He was too tired and out of shape to play vigorously, and the game was largely high jinks. He sat down and played the piano next to the racquetball court, and he sang a couple of gospel songs and a country song, 'Blue Eyes Crying in the Rain'. Then he returned to the house, and Billy Smith went upstairs with him to help him wash and dry his hair. Billy left at about 7 a.m., when Elvis went to bed. The last words Elvis said to him were 'Billy ... Son ... this is going to be my best tour ever.' Billy said Elvis was reading *The Scientific Search for the Face of Jesus*, by Frank O. Adams. A couple of days before, Larry Geller had brought Elvis some books he had requested, including this book about the Shroud of Turin, the relic reputed to be the shroud that holds the ghostly impression of Jesus' face. Still unable to sleep, Elvis got up and continued reading – perhaps one of the other books – in the bathroom while Ginger slept in the bedroom.

Early in the afternoon, she found him on the bathroom floor. Elvis had fallen over, his heart skipping off the track and seizing him. Ginger rushed to the telephone and summoned help from downstairs. Pandemonium tore through Graceland, with nine-year-old Lisa caught up in it. No one could believe he was dead. The ambulance arrived, and at the hospital, doctors worked on Elvis for an hour and a half before pronouncing him dead.

Officially, he died of cardiac arrhythmia. Fourteen drugs were found in his body – tranquillizers, painkillers, and antidepressants, drugs he took routinely, along with some heavy-duty painkillers he had taken after his dental work. The precise relationship of the drugs to his death is still debated, but he had clearly ruined his health with his numerous abuses.

Elvis seemed to have known for some time that he was

dying, and he asserted his acceptance of it, in part by his stubborn insistence on continuing to lead his life his own way. To Linda Thompson, he had acknowledged his self-destructiveness, but he would not stop. He was preoccupied with the anniversary of his mother's death. She died on 14 August, 1958, and his death came on 16 August, 1977.

'I'm coming to join you, son!' Vernon's grief-stricken wails were unearthly, like the chilling calls of the peacocks that once had paraded on the Graceland grounds. Now flower arrangements carpeted the lawn. Fifty thousand fans thronged the boulevard, and many were allowed through the gates to view Elvis's body in its copper casket in the front hallway of the mansion on the day prior to the funeral. The headline in the *Memphis Press-Scimitar* read 'A Lonely Life Ends on Elvis Presley Boulevard', and Tupelo's *Daily Journal* announced, 'The King Is Dead.' The shock travelled throughout the world, leading broadcast news programmes. Special tributes proliferated, and his music was everywhere.

The funeral was huge, with a long service in the living room at Graceland and music by Elvis's cherished gospel singers, and afterwards a procession of seventeen white limousines. Colonel Parker wore a baseball cap and seersucker pants to the funeral.

Elvis was entombed in a mausoleum near his mother's grave at Forest Hills Cemetery, but a few weeks later, after acts of attempted vandalism, his body was moved to the Meditation Garden at Graceland. His mother's remains were moved, too, and his father, after another heart attack, joined them two years later. Elvis's grandmother, Minnie Mae Presley, died in 1980 and was laid to rest among them. A plaque was added in honour of Elvis's missing twin, Jesse Garon.

Elvis remains one of the most popular of modern heroes, in spite of his failure to slay his internal dragons. He was haunted always by nightmares of rejection, especially the fear that he would lose his fans and thus his golden identity. Unprepared to handle the monumental onslaught of public attention, he dissipated much of his talent on the burden of his fame.

The public ate him alive. In mythology, the hero is often devoured – the Egyptian corn god Osiris was dismembered and spread around like fertilizer – sacrificed by the people for the fertility of the community, or perhaps because there is something dark, jealous, and possessive in the human heart that wants to destroy those who take our risks for us. Elvis, the consumer supreme, was consumed, both before and after his death.

Or, put it this way: he was struggling with the basic questions of life, with the glare of the spotlight blinding him. Elvis always behaved as if there were no limits. It was his genius, and his curse. His excess of aspiration spurred his worthiest achievements. When Elvis blended all the music he had ever heard and the opposing sides of his nature and the opposite races and classes of his region into one high-voltage eruption of music – wasn't this in itself a blatant excess? But it was brilliant. Shattering barriers musically and socially, indulging his appetites without restraint, and giving away thirteen pick-up trucks in one day – all of Elvis's extreme behaviour came out of the same impulse. His talent was so prodigious, his spirit so volatile and uninhibited, that he was able to embody for millions the rebel spirit in spite of his personal fears. Elvis tried his very best to understand his place in the world, but he was struggling with something too perplexing to grasp.

When it became apparent to Colonel Parker that his golden goose was dying, he hatched a marketing plan. He was on the phone to Vernon as soon as he learned of Elvis's death. Foreseeing that Elvis was worth as much dead as alive, he sought Vernon's signature to extend his management deal with Elvis. In a bright Hawaiian shirt, Parker soon arrived at Graceland. Vernon, in his grief, signed what in effect was an agreement for the Colonel to own Elvis in perpetuity, an arrangement overturned by the courts after Vernon's death. In the early eighties, the court, on evidence of 'collusion, fraud, misrepresentation, bad faith, and overreaching', voided all of Parker's claims, and it challenged the terms of the 1973 buyout of Elvis's valuable back catalogue. The Elvis Presley estate retained all post-1973 royalties.

In 1984, Priscilla, executor until Lisa came of age, turned Graceland into a profitable enterprise, ensuring Lisa's inheritance. Graceland, a real place where Elvis Presley and his parents and his grandmother lived and died and were buried, became by the end of the twentieth century the most visited private home in America.

ACKNOWLEDGEMENTS

ONE OF THE GREAT delights of writing this book was the chance to spend time in Memphis. I owe Cindy Hazen and Mike Freeman special thanks for extending to me and my husband the privilege of house-sitting, and pet-sitting, at their home for two weeks. Their home on Audubon Drive in Memphis was the house Elvis bought for his parents in 1956, the year he became famous. It was especially compelling to be there, because I consider the Audubon Drive house to be of major significance in Elvis's life. Possibly moving to a four-bedroom ranch house was the most exciting reward to the Presleys ever to come of Elvis's success. After that, everything became too complicated for them to experience the same thrill again. The house is much the same as it was in 1956, and Cindy and Mike have faithfully decorated it to match its appearance when Elvis lived there. The original wallpaper is emerging from peeling layers; the low brick-and-wrought-iron fence the Presleys installed still distinguishes the house, although the decorative musical notes have disappeared; the white-brick fireplace that appears in the famous photograph of Elvis in his gold-leaf suit still stands; the swimming pool is still in use. The oak and birch trees the Presleys planted now tower over the yard. Living there for two weeks helped put me in the frame of mind of Elvis and his parents in 1956 – the excitement of the new pool, the fans crowding in the carport, Gladys in her gleaming, modern kitchen, and Elvis lolling on the bed – surrounded by teddy bears – reading his fan mail. The dominant impression was a feeling for how far they had come in life.

After living on Audubon Drive for a year, the Presleys moved to a bigger place. An understanding of Elvis's dream, and how the Audubon Drive house was a stepping-stone along the way, is essential to understanding what Graceland meant to him. The people at Graceland kindly let me return again and again to tour the mansion and the museums, which contain such rich, evocative clues to Elvis's life – and the fulfilment of his ambition – that one visit was not enough. My thanks to Jack Soden, Bobby Davis, and La Vonne Gaw.

My main source was Peter Guralnick's monumental, definitive two-volume biography of Elvis – *Last Train to Memphis* and *Careless Love*. I turned to these books for certainty and assurance, relying on his thorough research into Elvis's career, his music, his life. And I thank him personally for his generous and enthusiastic guidance as I plunged into the minutiae of Elvis's life and music. He was able to advise me on the reliability of sources and some lines of enquiry to pursue. And he graciously reviewed the manuscript for accuracy, although I won't hold him responsible for my mistakes.

Some of the other books I paid close attention to:

Elvis Day by Day, by Peter Guralnick and Ernst Jorgensen, is an indispensable guide to the chronology of events in Elvis's life.

Alanna Nash's *Elvis Aaron Presley* contains interviews with three of the Memphis Mafia that were most helpful.

Elaine Dundy's *Elvis and Gladys* was especially useful in its portrait of Elvis's mother, as well as in its account of Elvis's early years in Tupelo.

Some other books that offered helpful insights into Elvis's early life: *Elvis's Man Friday* by Gene Smith, Elvis's cousin; and several books by Bill E. Burk, who knew Elvis in the early years and gathered photos and anecdotes from Tupelo and from Humes High School classmates.

Ernst Jorgensen's *Elvis Presley: A Life in Music* is a thorough chronology, with full interpretation of Elvis's recording sessions.

June Juanico's memoir *Elvis: In the Twilight of Memory* is a moving account of her relationship with Elvis during the heady summer of 1956. I am most appreciative of her gracious reply to my enquiries.

Egil Krogh's *The Day Elvis Met Nixon* is a precise account of Elvis's visit to the Oval Office in 1970, with photos to document the bizarre and memorable event.

Greil Marcus's 'Presliad', in *Mystery Train*, displays a breathtaking grasp of the energy and mystery and significance of Elvis's talent.

Elvis by Dave Marsh was especially valuable because of his deep understanding of Elvis's character – as a Southerner and as an American hero.

Elvis '56 by Alfred Wertheimer contains some of the most penetrating photographs of Elvis, with an account of Wertheimer's travels with Elvis. I pored over these photos at length, especially the series at Audubon Drive, in my attempt to imagine Elvis's life.

My Life with Elvis, by Becky Yancey, one of the secretaries at Graceland, gave some interesting and illuminating detail about life at Graceland, especially about the role of Elvis's father, Vernon.

My account of Elvis meeting the Beatles comes from varied sources, including *The Beatles Anthology* and Chris Hutchins's *Elvis Meets the Beatles*.

My gratitude extends to the individuals who welcomed my visits and helped me out in my quest to understand Elvis: Jack Reed Sr and Jack Reed Jr at Gum Tree Bookstore at Reed's Department Store in Tupelo, Mississippi; Leon Riley at the Tupelo Hardware Store, where Elvis bought his first guitar; Charles Reagan Wilson at the Center for Southern Culture Studies, Oxford, Mississippi; Jennifer Ford and Lee McWhite at the Special Collections at the Williams Library, University of Mississippi. Special thanks to Paul Yandell, who as a guitarist for the Louvin Brothers toured with Elvis in 1955–56. He supplied some anecdotes and eyewitness accounts of the early Elvis onstage – a period not documented on film.

Thanks also to Michael Bertrand, Erika Brady, Jerry Crutchfield, Allan Fesmire, Wade Hall, Beverly Halpern, Lamar Herrin, Aaron Hutchings, June Juanico, Greil Marcus, Dave Marsh, Guy Mendes, Corey and Cheryl Mesler, Alanna Nash, Christopher Shay, Charles K. Wolfe.

SELECTED SOURCES

BIBLIOGRAPHY

Bertrand, Michael. *Race, Rock, and Elvis*. University of Illinois Press, 2000.

Bova, Joyce, as told to William Conrad Nowels. *Don't Ask Forever: My Love Affair with Elvis*. Kensington Books, 1994.

Burk, Bill E. *Early Elvis: The Humes Years*. Red Oak Press, 1990.

—. *Early Elvis: The Sun Years*. Propwash Publishing, 1997.

—. *Early Elvis: The Tupelo Years*. Propwash Publishing, 1994.

Chadwick, Vernon, ed. *In Search of Elvis*. Westview Press/HarperCollins, 1997.

Clayton, Rose, and Dick Heard, eds. *Elvis Up Close*. Turner Publishing, 1994.

Curtin, Jim, with Renata Ginter. *Elvis: The Early Years: A 2001 Fact Odyssey*. Celebrity Books, 1999.

Dundy, Elaine. *Elvis and Gladys*. Macmillan, 1985.

Escott, Colin, and Martin Hawkins. *Good Rockin' Tonight: Sun Records and the Birth of Rock 'n' Roll*. St Martin's Press, 1991.

Geller, Larry, and Joel Spector with Patricia Romanowski. *'If I Can Dream': Elvis' Own Story*. Simon & Schuster, 1989.

Gregory, Neal, and Janice Gregory. *When Elvis Died*. Communications Press, 1980.

Guralnick, Peter. *Careless Love: The Unmaking of Elvis Presley*. Little, Brown, 1999.

—. *Last Train to Memphis: The Rise of Elvis Presley*. Little, Brown, 1994.

—, and Ernst Jorgensen. *Elvis Day by Day*. Ballantine Books, 1999.

Hopkins, Jerry. *Elvis*. Simon & Schuster, 1971.

Hutchins, Chris, and Peter Thompson. *Elvis Meets the Beatles*. Smith Gryphon, 1995.

Israel, Marvin. *Elvis Presley 1956*. Photographs by Marvin Israel. Edited and designed by Martin Harrison. Harry N. Abrams, 1998.

Jorgensen, Ernst. *Elvis Presley: A Life in Music: The Complete Recording Sessions*. St Martin's Press, 1998.

Juanico, June. *Elvis: In the Twilight of Memory*. Arcade Books, 1997.

Krogh, Egil 'Bud'. *The Day Elvis Met Nixon*. Pejama Press, 1994.

Logan, Horace, with Bill Sloan. *Elvis, Hank, and Me: Making Musical History on the Louisiana Hayride*. St Martin's Press, 1998.

Lomax, Alan. *The Land Where the Blues Began*. Dell, 1993.

Marcus, Greil. *Dead Elvis*. Doubleday, 1991.

—. *Mystery Train*. 4th rev. ed. Penguin, 1997.

Marsh, Dave. *Elvis*. Times Books, 1982.

Moore, Scotty, as told to James Dickerson. *That's Alright, Elvis: The Untold Story of Elvis's First Guitarist and Manager, Scotty Moore*. Schirmer, 1997.

Nash, Alanna, with Billy Smith, Marty Lacker, and Lamar Fike.

Elvis Aaron Presley: Revelations from the Memphis Mafia. HarperCollins, 1995.

Presley, Priscilla Beaulieu, with Sandra Harmon. *Elvis and Me.* G. P. Putnam's Sons, 1985.

Quain, Kevin, ed. *The Elvis Reader: Texts and Sources on the King of Rock 'n' Roll.* St Martin's Press, 1992.

Smith, Gene. *Elvis's Man Friday.* Light of Day Publishing, 1994.

Stern, Jane, and Michael Stern. *Elvis World.* Alfred A. Knopf, 1987.

Vellenga, Dirk, with Mick Farren. *Elvis and the Colonel.* Delacorte, 1988.

Wertheimer, Alfred, with Gregory Martinelli. *Elvis '56: In the Beginning.* Collier Books Macmillan, 1979.

West, Red, Sonny West, and Dave Hebler, as told to Steve Dunleavy. *Elvis, What Happened?* Ballantine Books, 1977.

Yancey, Becky, with Cliff Linedecker. *My Life with Elvis.* St Martin's Press, 1977.

VIDEOTAPES: PERFORMANCES AND DOCUMENTARIES

Elvis from the Waist Up

Elvis '56

The '68 Comeback Special

Elvis: The Great Performances

Elvis: One Night with You

Live at Madison Square Garden

Aloha from Hawaii

The Alternate Aloha

Elvis: That's the Way It Is, MGM, 1970

Elvis in Hollywood (AMC)

RECORDINGS

Playing with Fire: The Complete Louisiana Hayride Archive
The Complete Fifties Masters
The Complete Sixties Masters
The Complete Seventies Masters
Amazing Grace
Million Dollar Quartet
Suspicious Minds: The Memphis 1969 Anthology

FILMS

Love Me Tender
Loving You
Jailhouse Rock
King Creole
Flaming Star
Wild in the Country
Viva Las Vegas
Change of Habit

INDEX

· LIVES · LIVES · LIVES · L